D0834046

MINI ATLAS

of

BRITAIN

St Michael

This edition produced specially for Marks and
Spencer p.l.c., in 1993, by Bartholomew, a Division
of HarperCollins*Publishers* London

First published in 1987
Revised editions 1990,1991,1992,1993

ISBN 0 583 31504 6

Printed and bound in Great Britain

The contents of this edition of the *Mini Atlas of
Britain* are believed correct at the time of printing.
Nevertheless, the publisher can accept no
responsibility for errors or omissions, or for changes
in the detail given.

CONTENTS

BRITAIN

iv - v	Route Planning Maps
vi	Key to Maps
vii	Key to Symbols
1- 104	General Maps
105	London and the M25
106 - 137	Index

NORTHERN IRELAND

138	Key to Maps and Symbols
139 - 146	General Maps
147 - 149	Index

TOWN PLANS

150 - 157	Central London, Birmingham, Edinburgh, Glasgow, Leeds, Manchester

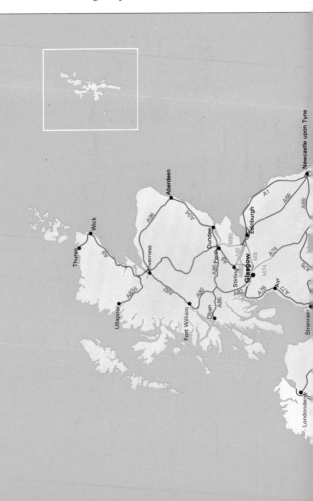

Page 103-104	**KEY**	Page 1-102

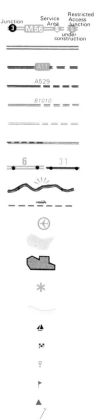

	motorway	
	dual carriageway	
	primary route	
	other "A" roads	
	"B" road	
	unclassified road	
	narrow road with passing places	
	distance in miles	
	gradient: viewpoint	
	car ferry	
	airport	
	scenic area	
	built up area	
	place of popular interest	
	sandy beach	
	sailing centre	
	motor racing circuit	
	race course	
	golf course	
	youth hostel	
	chairlift	
	spot height (feet)	
	national boundary	

Index

The index comprises of a selection of names and locations of towns and villages.

The reference number refers to the page, and the letter refers to the section of the map in which the index entry can be found, as divided into **a, b, c** and **d** thus:

a	b
c	d

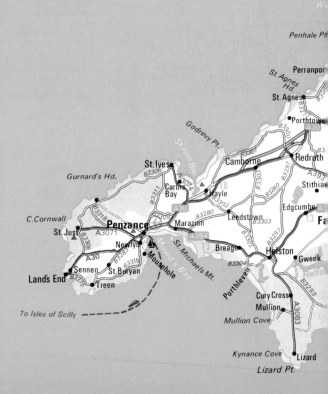

Penhale Pt.

Perranport

St. Agnes Hd.

St. Agnes

Porthtowan

Godrevy Pt.

Camborne

Redruth

St. Ives

Gurnard's Hd.

B3306

Carbis Bay

B3074

Hayle

Stithians

St. Ives Bay

B3301

B3300

B3297

A393

Edgcumbe

B3280

Leedstown

B3302

B3303

Fa

C. Cornwall

B3318

Penzance

Marazion

B3280

13

St. Just

A3071

A30

A394

3

Breage

B3297

Helston

Gweek

Newlyn

B3283

Mousehole

St. Michael's Mt.

Mount's Bay

Porthleven

B3304

Helfo

B3293

Land's End

Sennen

B3306

St. Buryan

B3315

A30

B3315

Treen

To Isles of Scilly

Cury Cross

Mullion

A3083

Mullion Cove

Kynance Cove

Lizard

Lizard Pt.

Bude
Stratton
A3072
Holsworthy
Highampton
Hatherleigh
Exbourne
A3079
A386
A388
Widemouth Bay
Clawton
Tamar
Whitstone
Okehampton
peak
A39
B3263
Ottery
Bridestowe
Sourton
A30
A386
Davidstow
Piperspool
Lifton
Launceston
Lydford
Downtown
DARTMOOR
Camelford
Fivelanes
S Petherwin
A388
Milton Abbot
A30
Dar
B3357
Bolventor 776
Postbridge
Fo
Bodmin
892
Upton Cross
Kellybray
Tavistock
Merrivale Br B3357
Two
703
Moor
A390
Princetown
Bridges
Fowey
St.Ive
Callington
Gunnislake
B3212
1100
Yelverton
in
13
Dobwalls
Liskeard
Bere Alston
Cornwood
38
A390
W.Taphouse
Tideford
A388
Toll
A386
Plympton
A38
Lostwithiel
St.Germans
Saltash
PLYMOUTH
B3259
Pelynt
Polbathic
Torpoint
Devonport
A379
Yealmpton
Modb
W.Looe E.Looe
A387
B3241
wey
Polperro
St.George's I.
Whitsand Bay
Rame Hd.
Newton Ferrers
Bigbury on Sea
Gribbin Hd.
Stoke Pt.
Bolt
Bigbury

To Santander   To Roscoff

Lundy

Ilfr
Bull Pt.
Mortehoe
Woolacombe B33
Morte Bay
Baggy Pt.
Saunton

Barnstaple or
Bideford Bay

Appledore

B3236
Bideford

Hartland Pt.
B3237 Clovelly
Hartland Quay
Hartland
B3248
Horns Cross
Ford
Monkleigh

A39

Sharpnose
Stibb Cross
B3227

Kilkhampton
B3254

Petro
Torrid

Bude
Stratton
A3072
Holsworthy
A388
Higham
A3079

Widemouth
Bay
Tamar
Clawton

Cambeak
Whitstone

A39

Boscastle B3263
Tintagel Hd.
30
Tintagel
B3263
Ottery
B3254
Bric
A30

Port Isaac
B3314
Davidstow
A395
Piperspool
Litton
Launceston
Milton Abbot

Camelford
Camel
Wolf
B3362

Polzeath
Fivelanes
S
Petherwin
A388

St. Kew
Highway
Bolventor
A30
776
Tamar

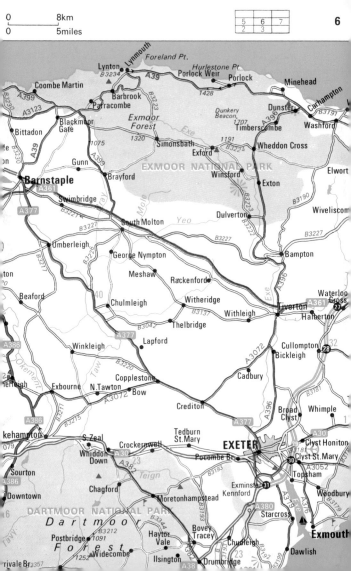

Dunster
Watchet
Putsham
Pawlett
Highbridge
Brue
Carhampton
B3191
A39
Timberscombe
Washford
Williton
Nether Stowey
Cannington
A38
23
Wheddon Cross
Crowcombe
Quantock Hills
B3839
A39
Greinton
Elworthy
QUANTOCK HILLS
Bridgwater
5
Exton
N. Petherton
24
Othery
22
B3190
Wiveliscombe
Bishops Lydeard
Durston
A361
Langport
Parrett
B3227
Milverton
Tone
Taunton
Nalcon Corner
Hambridge
Bampton
Wellington
A38
Ashill
S. Pether
Milverne
26
M5
A358
Blagdon
Horton
28
Waterloo Cross
27
Culmstock
Churchingford
B3170
Ilminster
Tiverton
A361
Halberton
Hemyock
A303
A358
31
Withleigh
Marsh
Chard
Mist
Cullompton
28
Upottery
Yarcombe
B3162
Bickleigh
A30
B3167
Cadbury
Broadwinds
A3072
B3181
A373
Talaton
Honiton
A35
Axminster
B3165
Whimple
17
B3177
B3161
A358
Charmouth
A35
Broad Clyst
B3174
Ottery St. Mary
A375
Colyford
A3070
Chide
EXETER
A30
Clyst Honiton
Newton Poppleford
A3052
Lyme Regis
We
Topsham
Clyst St. Mary
A3052
Sidford
B3174
Seaton
B3172
Beer
Exminster
31
B3176
Sidmouth
A380
A319
A376
Woodbury
B3178
Lyme Bay
Starcross
Exe
B3179
Budleigh Salterton
Chudleigh
23
Exmouth
B3192
Dawlish
A381
B3199
Teignmouth
Babbacombe Bay

15	16	17
8	9	10

Warminster
Heytesbury
Shrewton
Bulford
A303
Wherw
Longbridge Deverill
B390
Winterbourne
Stoke
B3083
A344
Amesbury
Cholderton
A343
Middle Wallop
A3057
Deptford
A303
Stapleford
Lopcombe
Corner
Stockbridge
Chicklade
A350
Wylye
A36
A345
A338
Test
Hindon
B3089
Barford
Wilton
A3094
Salisbury
A30
Dunbridge
A3057
Knoyle
Fovant
Whiteparish
ham
Shaftesbury
A30
Broad
Chalke
A354
Coombe
Bissett
A36
A27
Romsey
Rownh
Sixpenny
Handley
Woodyates
A338
B3080
Landford
B3078
Ower
Cadnam
Tott
A36 M
A336
Fontmell
Magna
B3081
Godshill
Fordingbridge
Stoney Cross
SOUTHAM
Cashmoor Corner
Cranborne
B3078
Ibsley
A31
Lyndhurst
A35
Stourpaine
Tarrant
Hinton
Verwood
Avon
New Forest
B3056
Forum
Horton
B3072
B3081
Ringwood
NEW FOREST
Brockenhurst
Beauli
B3055
B3092
West Moors
B3078
St. Leonards
B3347
B3055
Boldre
B3054
Almer
Wimborne Minster
Ferndown
A31
Tricketts Cross
A338
Sopley
B3058
Lymingt
Bere Regis
Morden
A350
A35
Kinson
Hinton
A35
Milton
A337
Downton
Lytchett Minster
Longfleet
A3049
Winton
Christchurch
B3058
Wool
hton
Wareham
Poole
BOURNEMOUTH
Boscombe
Christchurch Bay
Totland
Downs
E.Lulworth
Corfe
Castle
Studland
Alur Bay
The Needles
Freshwater
Kingston
A351
B3069
Swanage
Durlston Hd.
To Cherbourg
St. Albans Hd.

Purfleet Thurrock Cliffe Allhallows I. Grain
Woolwich Erith A2067 Tolly Tilbury Hoo of Sheerness
Dartford B2000 Grain B2001 Minste
Bexley A224 A2 Gravesend B228 Queenborough Sheppe
Sidcup B260 Shorne Strood Gillingham Medw
Chislehurst A25 Cobham Rochester Chatham Rainham Sittingbourne A2
Darningham Meopham A228 Sheen Str The Sw
Eynsford A21 Snodland Bredhurst M2 North A2000 10
Orpington A225 Kingsdown A20 Boxley A249 Doddington
Farnborough A225 Otford Wrotham Wrotham Heath Detling Newnh
Riverhead M26 A25 Seal Borough Gr. W. Malling Hollingbourne 15
Brasted Sevenoaks Mereworth Maidstone A20 Lenham
Westerham Hadlow Hale Yalding Harrietsham Charin
Crockham Hill A2042 Str.
Leigh Paddock Marden Headcorn Pluckley Great
Penshurst Wood Staplehurst Smarden Chart
Southborough Pembury Biddenden As
Ashurst Royal Goudhurst Sissinghurst Woodchurch
Groombridge Tunbridge Lamberhurst Cranbrook Tenterden
Hartfield Wells Frant Wadhurst Flimwell Hawkhurst Wittersham Brenz
Crowborough Ticehurst Rother Appledore
Weald Mayfield Burwash Northiam Peasmarsh
Uckfield Heathfield Robertsbridge Sedlescombe Playden Rye
Blackboys Brightling Battle Brede Winchelsea
East Hoathly Ninfield Westfield Hastings
Hallland Herstmonceux Hailsham Warbling St. Leonards
Ringmer Dicker Bexhill-on-Sea
Beddingham Wilmington Polegate Cooden
Alfriston Pevensey Willingdon

0 ___ 8km
0 ___ 5miles

To Vlissingen

Westgate on Sea
Birchington
Margate
Kingsgate
North Foreland
B2052
Broadstairs

...ch
eysdown
Herne Bay
Reculver
Whitstable
B2205
A299
I. of Thanet
Herne
Sarre
A253
Minster
Ramsgate
B255

...ham
A299
Blean
A290
Sturry
Stour
Richborough
Canterbury
A257
Wingham
A257
Littlebourne
Ash
Sandwich
A258
Richborough
Iham
A28
Bridge
B2046
Aylesham
Eastry
Deal
Walmer
B2057
DOWNS
Denton
A2
St.Margarets
at Cliffe
Elham
A260
Selstad
Alkham
Temple Ewell
South Foreland
To Oostende
D o w n s
Lyminge
Dover
A64
Sellindge
B2068
11
12
13
B2011
A20
Newingreen
A261
Folkestone
To Calais
Lympne
Sandgate
litary Canal
Hythe
isused)
A259
Ivychurch
Dymchurch
To Boulogne
nney
St Mary's Bay
B2075
Littlestone-on-Sea
Greatstone-on-Sea
Dungeness

S T R A I T   O F   D O V E R

Monmouth
Redbrook
Mitchel Troy
Raglan
Trellech
Llansoy
Tintern
Newnham
Forest of Dean
Saul
Blakeney
Bream
Lydney
Cambridg
Sharpness
Berkeley
Stone
S Michae
Blaenavon
Abertillery
Abersychan
Pontypool
Usk
Abergavenny
bw Vale
Newbridge
Abercarn
Cwmcarn
Cwmbran
Llandegfedd Res.
Chepstow
Thornbury
Alveston
Wic
Machen
Caerleon
Penhow
Caerwent
NEWPORT
Magor
Caldicot
Almondsbury
Aust
Chi
So
Castleton
St. Mellons
Filton
Winterbourne
Avonmouth
Gordano
Portishead
BRISTOL
Mangotsfield
Clifton
Kingswood
Oldland
Common
CARDIFF
enarth
Clevedon
Nailsea
Kenn
Flax Bourton
Whitchurch
Keynsham
BAT
Corston
Marksbury
vernock Pt.
Yatton
Redhill
Lulsgate
Congresbury
Pensford
Chew Stoke
Chew Valley
Worle
Churchill
Banwell
Sidcot
Axbridge
Blagdon
Mendip
Midsomer Norton
Radstock
Weston-super-Mare
Cheddar
Buckland Dinha
E. Brent
Sedgemoor
Wedmore
Oakhill
Nunney
Fr
Burnham
Mark
Wells
Shepton Mallet
Pilton
Wans
Highbridge
Pawlett
Cannington
Evercreech
Bridgwater
Greinton
Glastonbury
Street
W. Pennard
Bruton
wernock
water
ay
am
ther
wey

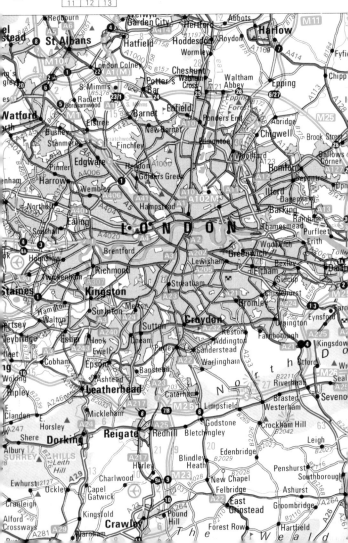

To Rosslare

Strumble Hd.

Fishguard Bay

Dinas Hd.

N

Goodwick

Fishguard

A487

Scleddau

B4313

A40

Mathry

A487

B4313

Letterston

Wolf's
Castle

B4330

Tufto

St.David's
Hd.

B

Solva

St.David's

Newgale

Ramsey I.

W. Cleddau

A487

B4329

St. Brides Bay

Haverfordwest

A40

Rot
W

Broad Haven

B4341

B4327

Canaston Br.

Skomer

St Brides

B4327

Johnston

A4076

A477

A4075

Grassholm

Milford
Haven

Steynton

To Rosslare Skokholm

Dale

St. Ann's Hd.

Milford Haven

Neyland

B4325

Burton

Pembroke
Dock

Pembroke

Lamph

Angle

B4320

St.
Petrox

B4584

B4319

Linney Hd.

St. Govans Hd.

Ynys Lochtyn
Llangranog
Synod Inn
Ystrad Aeron
Temple Bar
Llangybi
Aberporth
B4333
Sarnau
Cribyn
Lampeter
-Sea
Cardigan
B4487
Ffostrasol
Llanwnen
A475
Blaenporth
Rhyd-Owen
Llechryd
Horeb
Llandyssul
Llanybyther
A482
Bridell
Newcastle
Emlyn
Boncath
Gwyddgrug
Llansawel
Crymmych
Talley
Lla
Trelech
B4333
Cynwyl Elfed
Llanboidy
Llandissilio
Carmarthen
Llanegwad
Llandeil
Whitland
A40
St.Clears
15
Llanarthney
Llandybie
Red Roses
Laugharne
Llanddarog
Porth-y-Rhyd
Cross
Bryn
Llanddowror
Llandyfaelog
Tumble
Hands
Amman
Pendine
A4066
Ferryside
Pontyates
Pont Abraham
Saundersfoot
Kidwelly
Llanon
Hendy
Pontardulais
Tenby
Pembrey
Llanelli
Llwchwr
Mor
Caldy I.
Burry Port
Llanmadoc
SWANSEA
Llangennith
Upr. Killay
Black Pill
Llanddewi
Bishopston
Mumbles
Worms Hd.
Rhosili
Oxwich
Port Eynon
Oxwich Bay

To Cork (Summer Only)

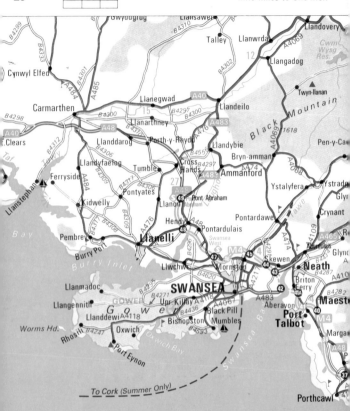

Aberystwyth
Goginan
Ponterwyd
A44
Rheidol
Pentrebont
B4340
Devils Br.
A4120
B4343
B4574
A4485
Llanilar
B4575
Ystwyth
Ysbyty Ystwyth
B4337
Llanrhystyd
Lledrod
Llansanffraid
Bronnant
Ystrad
Meurig
A4340
Pontrhydfendigaid
A487
Cross
B4578
Inn
B4577
A485
B4343
Aberaeron
B4457
Aberarth
B4516
Tregaron
b
New Quay
A482
B4342
B4342
38
A486
Ystrad Aeron
B4337
m
Llyn
Synod Inn
B4338
Temple Bar
Llangybi
A485
Teifi
Brianne
Resr
ch
Cribyn
A485
B4343
a
Llanwrt
Sarnau
B4334
B4459
Lampeter
37
B4571
Ffostrasol
A486
Llanwnen
A475
C
4333
Rhyd-Owen
B4459
A482
Horeb
B4337
Llanybyther
B4335
Llandysul
A485
Pumpsaint
Cilycwm
A4069
A484
A486
B4336
A483
Llandovery
B4459
Gwyddgrug
Llansawel
B4310
Cwm
B4299
B4337
Wysg
Res
B4333
Talley
Llanwrda
A40
12
A4069
Cynwyl Elfed
Llangadog
A484
B4302
A484
A301
Twyn-llanan
Llanegwad
A40
Black
Mountain
Carmarthen
B4300
15
B4297
A300
Llandeilo
A48
A483
Llanarthney
A476
1618
Llanddarog
B4310
Llandybie
Pen-y-Cae
Clears
B4312
Porth-y-Rhyd
A4069
A40
Llandyfaelog
B4455
Bryn-amman
A474
A
Taf
B4309
Tumble
Cross
B4297
Ammanford
A483
Ferryside
B4317
Hands
27
Ystradg
Pontyates
Llanon
Pont Abraham
Ystalyfera
Glyn
Kidwelly
49
Llanstephan
Pontardawe
Crynant

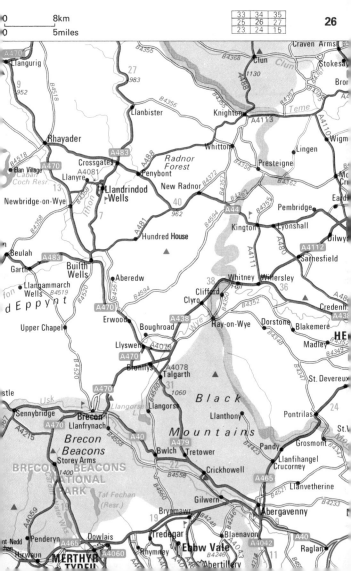

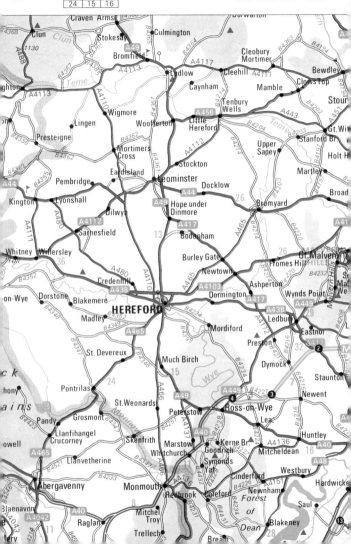

36	37	38
28	29	30
16	17	18

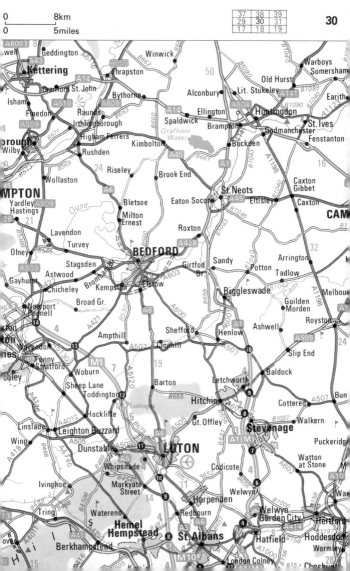

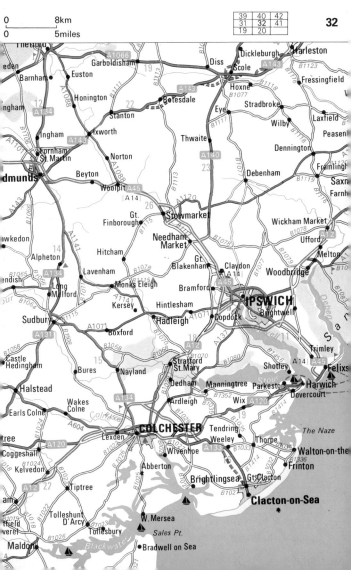

8km
5miles

A5104
Dee
Corwen
28
A5
A483
A542
Llangollen
A539
Ruabon
B5476
Overton
A539
A525
Marchwiail
Bangor
B5069
Malpas
Moss
A525
Whitchurch
A5

Glyn-Ceiriog
B4500
Chirk
A495
Hanmer
A495
Tilstock
A41
Tern

Dyffryn Ceiriog
B4500
A4519
Gobowen
A528
Ellesmere
Welshampton
B5476
Preees
A49

gynog
A4580
Whittington
A495
Oswestry
A4083
B4580
W. Felton
B4397
Burlton
B4397
Harmerhil
B5476
Wem 20
Preston
Brockhurst
B5063
Shawbu

Llanfyllin
A495
B4393
Llanymynech
A4083
A5
Baschurch
Harmerhil
Hadnall
A53
High
Ercall
Battlefield

yn
A490
Meifod
A495
Nesscliff
A5
B5062
A528
5062

A458
Welshpool
A483
Middletown
Buttington
Long
Mountain
Worthen
Westbury
B4386
A458
A49
Atcham
SHREWSBURY
We
A4380
Wroxete
B4380
The

nfair
nion
A458
B4385
B4390
Garthmyl
A483
B4388
Marton
B4386
Chirbury
A490
Minsterly
Dorrington
Cound
A458

wtown
89
A483
A489
Kerry
Sarn
Montgomery
A489
A488
14
Ratlinghope
B4370
Church
Stretton
Hope
Bowdler
B4371
SHROPSHIRE
HILLS
Shipton
B4378
Wenlock Edge

olfair
A483
Kerry Hill
Bishops Castle
Marshbrook
A489
B4385
B4370
FOREST
Munslow
Pedlar's
Rest
Ditton Priors
Cleobury North

Clun
Forest
B4368
Clun
1130
Clun
Craven Arms
B4368
Stokesay
A49
Culmington
B4364

B4355
B4356
A488
983
27
Llanbister
Knighton
A4113
Bromfield
Teme
A4113
Ludlow
A4117
Cle
Caynham

Llanbister
A4110
Wigmore
We
Ten

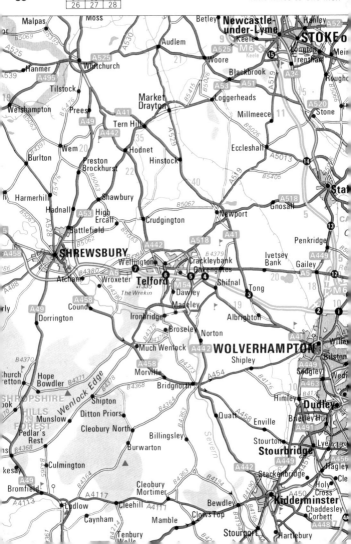

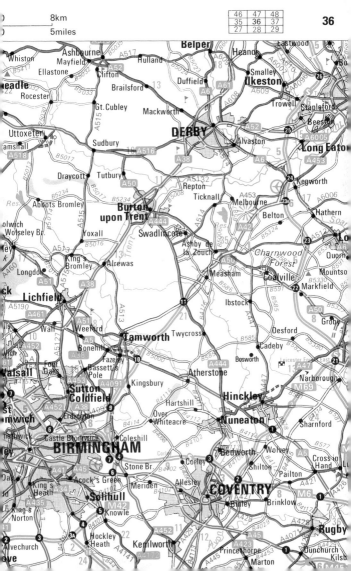

THE

WASH

6
A52 Benington

ston

Brancaster

NORFO

Hunstanton

Burnham

B1153

A1

Heacham

Docking

B1155

B1355

B1454

Holbeach
Marsh

Snettisham

B1155

B1454

43

Gedney Drove
End

Wolferton

Dersingham

A479

B1153

E. Rudham

A10

4

A17

B1359

Holbeach

Long
Sutton

Sutton Br.

Flitcham

Harpley

B1440

Castle
Rising

Great
Massingham

Sth. Wootton

A148

B1165

A1101

Tydd St. Mary

King's Lynn

A17

Gaywood

Gayton

Litcha

1079

B1145

Sutton
St. James

Terrington
St. Clement

A149

Middleton

Newton

B1165

St. John's
Highway

A47

E. Winch

16

W

dney Hill

Setchey

Narborough

A10

13

Nene

Ouse

Nar

Necton

B1169

Wisbech

11

Sth. Runcton

A1122

Swaffham

B1077

Guyhirn

B1411

13

A1065

21

A141

Outwell

A1122

Stradsett

Hilborough

B1101

B1094

Downham
Market

Stoke Ferry

March

B1098

Nordelph

A1101

Hilgay

B1160

Wissey

T h

B1099

Southery

Methwold

A134

B1388

Mundford

B1093

Doddington

Old Bedford

New Bedford

18

Feltwell

B1386

32

Cro

B1077

A10

Weeting

F e n s

35

Chatteris

B1411

Littleport

A1101

Brandon

Thetford

A142

Lark

Lakenheath

A1065

B1106

s

rsham

Sutton

Ely

B1382

Beck
Row

Elveden

Barnhan

Haddenham

Wilburton

Stretham

Isleham

Mildenhall

20

Icklingham

earith

A1123

13

B1112

Willingham

Soham

B1102

Barton
Mills

Lackford

A134

ottenham

Cam

Fordham

A11

B1098

Little Ouse

Blakeney   Cley   Weybourne   Sheringham
W. Runton   Cromer
Overstrand
Ikey
A149
A148

Letheringsett
Binham
Holt
Roughton
Thorpe Market
Mundesley
Paston
alsingham
B1388
B1110
Edgefield Green
Gunton
A149
B1150
Happisburgh

Saxthorpe
N. Walsham
B1145
Palling
Waxha
ham
37
B1067
Aylsham
Stalham
A149
B1151
Hor
Guist
Cawston
Marsham
Bure
Catfield
The
25
B1354
B1150
B1151
Martham
Reepham
A140
Coltishall
Hoveton
N.
Elmham
Bawdeswell
B1145
Horstead
B1354
A1062
B115
B1147
Attlebridge
Wroxham
B1152
Wensum
Horsham
Broads
A1062 Hil
E.
Dereham
Hockering
Drayton
A1067
Ranworth Walsham
A1149

Honingham
A1074
Thorpe
20
Bure
A1075
B1135
Easton
Blofield
Acle
Gor
B1108
Yare
NORWICH
Trowse Newton
Yare
Hethersett
A11
A146
Kimberley
Swardeston
B1140
Reedham
A1
B1108
Wymondham
Swainsthorpe
Hingham
B1113
Loddon
Caston
B1077
A140
Haddiscoe
Ashwellthorpe
B1135
B1332
Wavene
arling
Attleborough
Long
Stratton
Hempnall
Beccles
A1
20
B1332
Nth. C
B1111
New
Buckenham
Bungay
B1062
Mettingham
A145
B112
E.Harling
B1134
Pulham
A143
19
Homersfield
A144
Brampton
A1
Kenninghall
B1077
B1134
A12
Dickleburgh
Harleston
Halesworth
A1066
Diss
Scole
A143
B1123
Redon
oldisham
B113
Hoxne
B1118
Fressingfield
Walpole
Blythburgh
A105
B111
Botesdale
A143
B1077
Eye
Stradbroke
Bramfield
43
Stanton
B1117
Wilby
Laxfield
B138
worth
Peasenhall

32	32	39
32	41	40

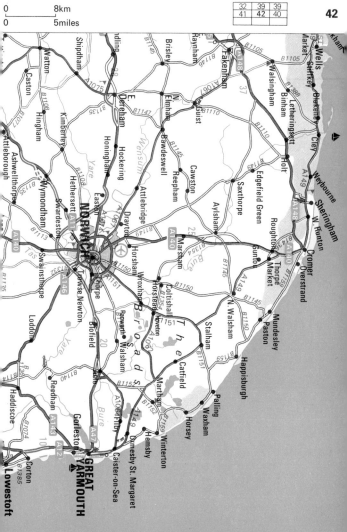

32	39	39
41	42	40

0 — 8km
0 — 5miles

Watton
Shipdham
Caston
Hingham
Kimberley
Ashwellthorpe
Wymondham
Attleborough
Swardeston
Hethersett
Easton
Drayton
NORWICH
Swainsthorpe
Lakeham
Lewise Newton
Thorpe
Loddon
Blofield
Reedham
Haddiscoe
Corton
Lowestoft

E. Dereham
Hockering
Honingham
N. Elmham
Bawdeswell
Reepham
Attlebridge
Cawston
Guist
Brisley
Raynham
Fakenham
Walsingham
Binham

Saxthorpe
Aylsham
Edgefield Green
Roughton
Gunton
Thorpe Market
Holt
Letheringsett
Cley

Wells
Stiffkey
Blakeney
Weybourne
W. Runton
Sheringham
Cromer
Overstrand

Marsham
Horsham
Wroxham
Coltishall
Horstead Newton
Rackheath
Ranworth
S. Walsham
Catfield
Stalham
N. Walsham
Paston
Mundesley
Happisburgh

Broads
The Broads
Martham
Winterton
Horsey
Palling
Waxham
Hemsby
Ormesby St. Margaret
Caister-on-Sea
GREAT YARMOUTH
Gorleston

Yare
Tas
Bure
Wensum
Yare

Carmel Hd.

Poir

Cemaes
Bay

Amlwch

A5025

B5112

Llanfeathlu

Ala
Res

Llanerchymedd

Llanallgo

To Dublin & Dun Laoghaire

A5025

B5109

A n g l e s e y

Holyhead

Valley

Bryngwran

Gwalchmai

Llange

A5114

Holy I.

A5

Llanf

Baerw

Rhosneigr

Llanfaelog

21

A4080

Aberffraw

Bethel

B4421

B4419

Newborough

B4419

Caernarfon

C a e r n a r f o n

B a y

A499

Pen-y

Llanll

Clynnog-fawr

A487

20

Llanaelhaearn

Nefyn

B4417

B4411

D

L l e y n   P e n i n s u l a

A499

B4354

A499

Llangwnnadl

B4415

Pwllheli

Cri

Sarn Mellteyn

B4413

A499

Llanbedrog

Aberdaron

Abersoch

T r e m a d o

B a y

Porth
Neigwl

St.Tudwals Is.

Bardsey I.

Pencilan Hd.

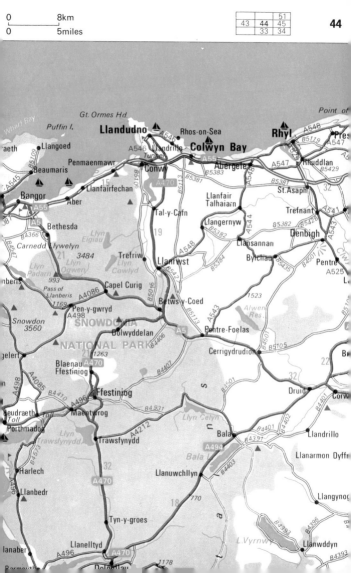

BURY
Heywood
Newhey
Marsden
Meltham
Kirkburton
A6
Radcliffe
Whitefield
Boyton
OLDHAM
Saddleworth
Holmfirth
Denby Dale
Silkston
Middleton
Mossley
A635
A6024
Ingbirchworth
Thurlstone
Penisto
Salford
MANCHESTER
Ashton-under-Lyne
Stalybridge
Woodhead
Stocksbridge
Stretford
M602
Denton
Hyde
Hollingworth
Glossop
Reservoirs
Ladybower Resr
SHE
Withington
Romiley
A626
A624
Hayfield
The Peak 2088
Castleton
Bamford
Ecc
STOCKPORT
Marple
New Mills
Ch.
Cheadle
Bramhall
Hazel Grove
Poynton
Disley
Whaley Bridge
Chapel-en-le-Frith
Peak Forest
Hathersage
Calver
Baslow
Wilmslow
Mobberley
Alderley Edge
Bollington
Tideswell
PEAK DISTRICT
CH
Peover
Chelford
Buxton
1690
Bakewell
Chats Park
Row
Macclesfield
Siddington
NATIONAL PARK
Monyash
Youlgreave
Holmes Chapel
Allgreave
1534
Longnor
Winster
Matlock Bath
Bosley
Upr. Hulme
Hartington
Warslow
Cromford
Wirksworth
Longton
Biddulph
Leek
Bottom Ho.
Tissington
Lawton
Kidsgrove
Endon
A520
Cheadleton
Ipstones
Tunstall
Burslem
Wetley Rocks
Whiston
Ashbourne
Hulland
Newcastle-under-Lyme
Keele
Hanley
STOKE on TRENT
Mayfield
Ellastone
Clifton
Brailsford
Blackbrook
Fenton
Trentham
Meir
Cheadle
Rocester
Roughclose
Checkley
Gt. Cubley
Mackwer
Hiderstone
Uttoxeter

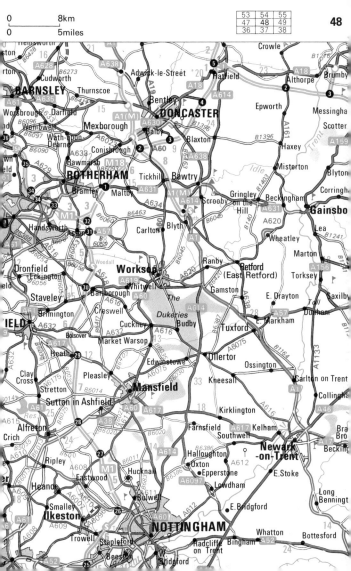

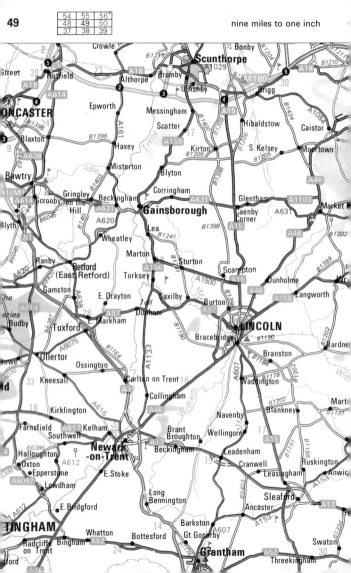

Millom
Askam
Ulverston
B5281
Cartmel
Grange over Sands
Arnside
Silverdale
Cark
BARROW-IN-FURNESS
Dalton
Bardsea
A590
A5087
Walney I.
Gleaston
Morecambe Bay
Carnfor
Slyne
Morecambe
A5105
Rampside
Foulney I.
Heysham
A589
A598
Hilpsford Pt.
To Douglas
To Douglas (Summer Only)
Lune
Galgate
Cockerham
A588
13
Fleetwood
Rossall Pt.
Pilling
Preesall
Garstan
A587
Cleveleys
A585
St. Michaels on Wyre
A586
Poulton-le-Fylde
Singleton
A584
A586
23
Fylde
Bro
M55
BLACKPOOL
Kirkham
3
A583
B5259
A584
A585
17
Warton
Lytham St. Annes
Ribble
Longton
Tarleton
18
A565
SOUTHPORT
B5244
Eccles
A570
Rufford
A59
Burscough Br.
A520
Ainsdale
A567
A565
Ormskir
B5195
Formby
A570
B5240
30
A59
20
Maghull

Isle of Man inset:
To Belfast & Stranraer
Pt. of Ayre
Bride
Ramsey
Ballaugh
A3
Sulby
Kirk Michael
Snaefell 2034
Peel
Laxey
A2
Grosb
A1
Onchan
ISLE OF MAN
A5
Douglas
Niarbyl B.
To Heysham
Port Erin
Santan Hd.
To Fleetwood
Castletown
To Liverpool
Port St. Mary
Calf of Man
To Dublin (Summer Only)

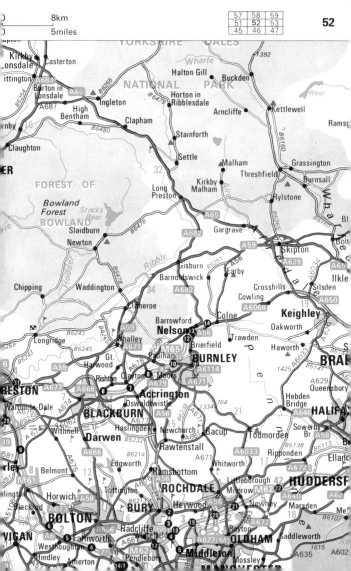

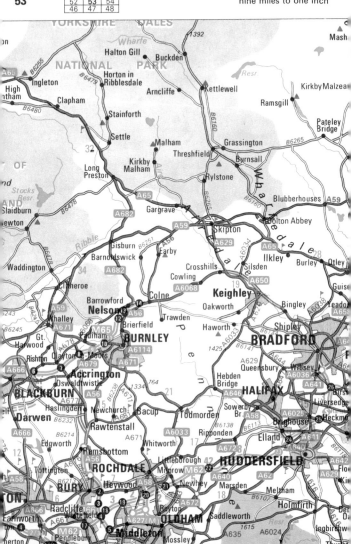

A1039
B1281 18
Filey
Ikton A1039 Muston
n Hunmanby
d s Reighton
es
North Burton *B1229* Bempton
A165 *B1255*
Rudston *B1255* *B1259* Flamborough
B1253 **Flamborough Hd.**
ft
m **Bridlington**
Carnaby Hilderthorpe
Burton *Bridlington*
A166 Agnes
Nafferton *Bay*
at **Driffield**
B1249 Skipsea
B1249
swick N. Frodingham Atwick
A165
Brandesburton **Hornsea**
30 *B1244*
field Leven *B1243* Mappleton
1035 Long
Riston
everley Aldbrough
B1238 *B1242*
Cottingham A165 Sproatley
Haltemprice *B1239* *B1240* Roos
HULL Withernsea
ssle Heddon *B1362*
New Holland 41033
Barrow Ottringham
Thornton Patrington *B1445*
Curtis Easington
A1077
5 Ulceby Immingham Kilnsea
A18 *B1210* A160
A180
GRIMSBY
A18 *A7099*
Scartho **Cleethorpes**
A1 Laceby Humberston
Waltham

Holderness

Humber

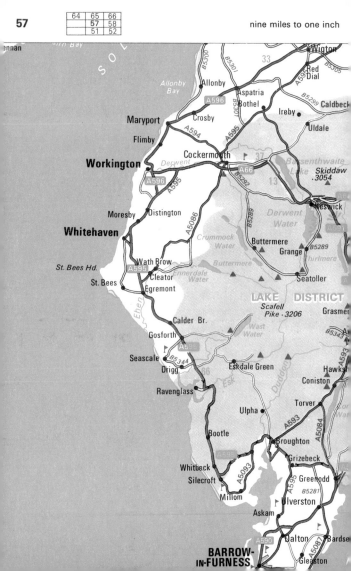

ennan

Solway Bay

SOLWAY

Allonby Bay

Allonby

Aspatria

Bothel

B5300

B5301

B5301

Wigton

Red Dial

Caldbeck

A596

Ireby

Uldale

Maryport

Crosby

A594

A596

Flimby

B5291

Cockermouth

Workington

Derwent

A66

A5292

Bassenthwaite Lake

Skiddaw
·3054

A596

A595

B5289

Derwent
Water

Keswick

Moresby

Distington

A5086

Crummock
Water

B5289

Whitehaven

St. Bees Hd.

A595

Wath Brow

Cleator

St. Bees

Egremont

Ehen

Ennerdale
Water

Buttermere

Buttermere

Grange

B5289

Thirlmere

Seatoller

LAKE   DISTRICT

Scafell
Pike ·3206

Grasmere

Calder Br.

Gosforth

A595

West
Water

B5343

Seascale

B5344

Drigg

A66

Eskdale Green

Duddon

Esk

Coniston

Hawkshe

Ravenglass

Ulpha

Torver

A593

A5084

Bootle

A595

Broughton

Grizebeck

Whitbeck

A5093

Greenodd

Silecroft

A595

B5281

Millom

Ulverston

Askam

A590

**BARROW-
IN-FURNESS**

Dalton

A5087

Bardsea

Gleaston

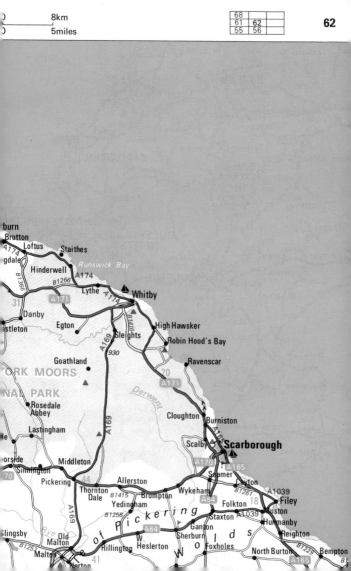

8km
5miles

burn
Brotton
Loftus   Staithes
A174
gdale
Hinderwell   A174
B1266
B1366   *Runswick Bay*
A171   Lythe   Whitby
31
Danby   Egton
astleton   High Hawsker
A169   Sleights   Robin Hood's Bay
930
Goathland   Ravenscar
RK MOORS
20
NAL PARK   A171
Rosedale   *Derwent*
Abbey
Lastingham   Cloughton   Burniston
rside   Middleton   Scalby
Simington   **Scarborough**
70   A170   A165
Pickering   Seamer
Thornton   Allerston   Cayton   A1039
Dale   B1415 Brompton Wykeham   Filey
Yedingham   A64 Folkton 18 Hunston
B1258   Staxton   A1039 Hunmanby
A169   Ganton   Reighton
lingsby Old   W. Sherburn   B1229
B125 Malton   Rillington Hesterton Foxholes North Burton Bempton
Malton   Norton   A165
41   B1
Pickering
Wolds

Ailsa Craig

Girvan

New Dailly
Old Dailly

B741

B734

C a r r

Lendalfoot

A77

A714

Barr

1281
Polmaddie
Hill

Colmonell B734

Stinchar

Barrhill

Cree

Ballantrae

Tig

559

B7027

A714

Beneraird
1435

L. Dorna

Glen App

G a l

Bladnoch

To Larne

Corsewall Pt.

Kirkcolm

B738

A718

B738

Loch Ryan

Cairnryan

A77

To Belfast

Luce

Tarf

The Moors

58

Leswalt

B738

New Luce

The Rinns

Stranraer

Cas.Kennedy

A75

Glenluce

Kir

A77

B7077

Portpatrick

B7042

A716

B7084

A747

Machrum

B7005

Stoneykirk

Sandhead

Galloway

A716

**Kirk of
Mochrum**

Port William

L u c e

B a y

Port Logan

A716

B7065

Drummore

B7041

Mull of Galloway

Hills

Sanquhar
Mennock 2403
Mennock
A102
Dalveen P.
Daer Resr.
Durisdeer
Carronbridge
Penpont
Thornhill
Tynron
A76
Closeburn
oniaive A702
Dunscore
L. Urr
Parkgate
Templand
Ae
Lochmaben
A709
Locharbriggs
A701
Maxwelltown
Torthorwald
Dumfries
A75
Dalton
Crocketford
Mouswald
Springholm
Glencaple
Bankend
Clarencefield
A711
ossmichael
New Abbey
Criffel
· 1866
Dalbeattie
B793
Kirkbean
Palnackie
B736
Kippford
A710
encairn
ght
Dundrennan
Auchencairn Bay

Moffat
Capplegill
Ettrick Pen
· 2268
B709
1096
Beattock
A701
B7020
Dryfe
Boreland
Corrie
Common
B7068
Milk
Lockerbie
A74
B725
Ecclefechan
B723
Kirkpatrick
Fleming
B7224
Gretna Gr
Annan
Cummertrees
Dornock
Eastrig
Port
Carlisle

Moricambe
Bay
B5307
Kirkbride
Silloth
Newton
Arlosh
B5302
Oulton
Beckfoot
Abbey
Town
B5302
Wigt
B5300
B5301
Red
Dial
33
Allonby
Bay
Allonby
Aspatria
A596
Ca
Bothel
Ireby
B5299
Uldale
Maryport
Crosby
Flimby
A594
A595
Cockermouth

SOLWAY FIRTH

Southerness
Pt.

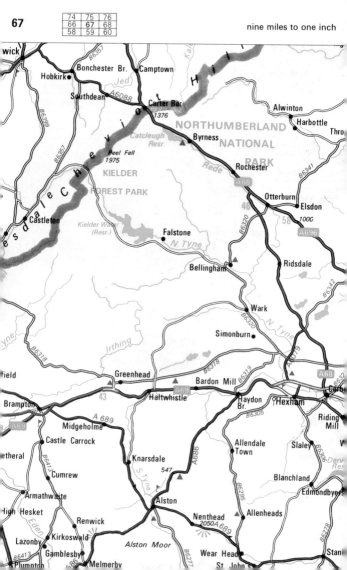

wick

Hobkirk

Bonchester Br. Camptown

Jed

Southdean A6088

Carter Bar
1376

Cheviot Hills

Alwinton

Harbottle

Thro

NORTHUMBERLAND

Byrness

Catcleugh
Resr.

NATIONAL

Peel Fell
1975

Rede

Rochester
A68

PARK

B6341

KIELDER

Otterburn

46

58 100C

FOREST PARK

A696

Castleton

Kielder Water
(Resr.)

Falstone

B6320

Elsdon

N. Tyne

Bellingham

Ridsdale

B6342

Wark

B6320

N. Tyne

Simonburn

A68

Irthing

B6318

field

Greenhead

B6378

B6319

A68

B637

Tyne

Brampton

A69

43

Haltwhistle

Bardon Mill

A69

Haydon
Br.

B6305

Corb

Hexham

A689

Midgeholme

Riding
Mill

Castle Carrock

Allendale
Town

Slaley

B6306 Derv
Res

etheral

B6413

Knarsdale

A686

547

Blanchland

Edmondbyers

Cumrew

S. Tyne

B6278

B6295

Armathwaite

Alston

Blanchland

High Hesket

Nenthead
2050 A689

Allenheads

Allendale

Renwick

Eden

Kirkoswald

Alston Moor

B6277

Wear Head

St. John's

Stan

Lazonby

Gamblesby

B6413

Plumpton Melmerby

0 8km

0 5miles

Longhoughton

Alnwick

Lesbury

Alnmouth

Warkworth

Alnmouth Bay

ngham

Newton on the Moor

Amble

Felton

Acklington

Coquet

gframlington

Druridge Bay

A1068

Longhorsley

Ugham

Ellington

Netherwitton

Longhirst

Ashington

rn

Morpeth

Mitford

Newbiggin-by-the-Sea

Whalton

Bedlington

Stannington

A1

Blyth

elsay

Cramlington

Blyth

Seaton Delaval

Ponteland

Whitley Bay

Earsdon

Killingworth

Tynemouth

Heddon on the Wall

Gosforth

Longbenton

Wallsend

S.Shields

To Bergen

To Stavanger

To Göteborg

To Esbjerg

Ryton

NEWCASTLE UPON TYNE

Jarrow

Hebburn

Newburn

Blaydon

Gateshead

Prudhoe

Whickham

Felling

Boldon

Whitburn

To Hamburg
(Summer Only)

Washington

SUNDERLAND

Ebchester

Birtley

Stanley

Chester-le-Street

New Seaham

Ryhope

Consett

Houghton-le-Spring

Hetton le Hole

Seaham

Lanchester

Witton Gilbert

A167

Easington

DURHAM

Satley

Haswell

Peterlee

Law

Brancepeth

Brandon

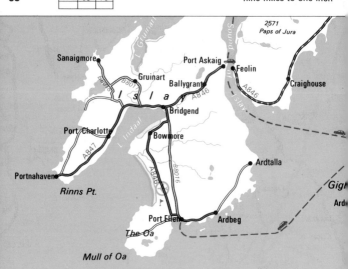

Sanaigmore

Port Askaig • Feolin

Gruinart

Ballygrant • Craighouse

I s l a y

Bridgend

Port Charlotte

A847

Bowmore

L Indaal

Portnahaven

Rinns Pt.

Ardtalla

A846

B8016

Port Ellen • Ardbeg

The Oa

Mull of Oa

2571
Paps of Jura

Gigh

Ard

Bel

Machriha

Rathlin I.

Mull of Kinty

8km
5miles

Kilmory

L. Caolisport

Tighnabruaich
Kames
Colintraive

Dunoon

Innellan

A83

K n a p d a

Tarbert
W. Tarbert

B8024

W. Tarbert

Kennacraig
Whitehouse
B8001

Skipness

B842

Clachan

Crossaig

Claonaig

Lochranza

A841

Summer Only

Ardlamont Pt.

Inchmarnock

Sd of Bute

Port
Bannatyne

Rothesay
Ascog

A844

A886

A844

Gt.
Cumbrae I.
Millport
B896

Kilchattan

Lit.
Cumbrae I.

Inv
We

Skel

Lar

Fa

33

A78

B7

W.

Tayinloan

Killean

Carradale
Dippen

Glenbarr

Saddell

Kilchenzie

Campbeltown
Davaar I.

Southend

Sanda

A83

Pirnmill

Goat Fell
2866

A841

A r r a n

Blackwaterfoot

Lagg

Sannox
Corrie

Brodick

B880

Lamlash

Holy I.

A841

Whiting Bay

Pladda I.

Seamill

Ardrossan

F I R T

O F

C L Y D

Culzean Cast

Maidens

Turnberry

Girvan

Ailsa
Craig

Kilbrannan Sound

t y r e

 Kana

Dunoon

GRE

Port G

Tighnabruaich

Colintraive

Innellan

Inverkip

Kames

Wemyss Bay

Port Bannatyne

Skelmorlie

Tarbert

A83

W. Tarbert

Ardlamont Pt.

Rothesay

Ascog

Gt. Cumbrae I.

Largs

Lochwin

Kennacraig

Whitehouse

B8001

Inchmarnock

Millport

Kilbirnie

Skipness

Lachan

Sd. of Bute

Kilchattan

Fairlie

Dalry

Crossaig

Claonaig

Lochranza

Lit. Cumbrae I.

W. Kilbride

Au

A78

Kilbrannan Sound

Pirnmill

Sannox

Corrie

Goat Fell 2866

Seamill

Kilwinning

Ardrossan

Stevens

Brodick

B880

Saltcoats

Or

Irvine Bay

rradale

ene

Arran

Lamlash

F I R T H

Blackwaterfoot

A841

Holy I.

O F

Troon

Whiting Bay

C L Y D E

Prestw

Lagg

AYR

Pladda I.

Culzean Castle

Maybole

A7

Maidens

Turnberry

Kirkoswald

B741

Ailsa Craig

New Dailly

Old Dailly

Girvan

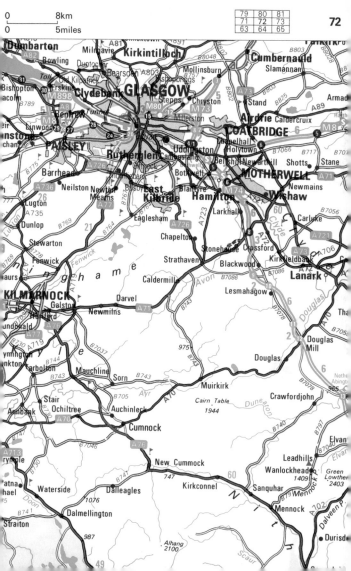

Milngavie A81 Kirkintilloch Cumbernauld Slamannan Falkirk Pumbuilt

Bowling Duntocher Mollinsburn B803 B825

Old Kilpatrick A803 Bearsden Bishopbriggs B757 B803 B825 Armadale Torbr Bal

Clydebank M898 GLASGOW Stepps Chryston Stand A89 Whitbu

Benhraw M80 Millerston Airdrie Caldercruix M8

PAISLEY Rutherglen Uddingston COATBRIDGE Chapelhall 5

Barrhead Cambuslang Bothwell Bellshill Newarthill Shotts Stane B7010

Neilston Newton Blantyre MOTHERWELL Newmains Wilson

Mearns East Kilbride Hamilton Wishaw A71

Blantyre M74 Larkhall Carluke B7056

Eaglesham Chapelton Stonehouse Crossford Kirkfieldbank Carstairs Libberton

Strathaven Blackwood Lanark A70

Caldermill B7086 B7086 A73

Darvel Lesmahagow Thankerton Tinto 2335 Symng

Newmilns A71 B743 975 Douglas Mill B7055

Mauchline Sorn B743 Douglas Nether Abington 965

Muirkirk Crawfordjohn Abington Crawfo

Auchinleck Cairn Table 1944 A70 B197

Cumnock B7040 Elvanfoot Bea Sur

A76 B7046 Leadhills A702 A7

New Cummock Wanlockhead 1409 Green Lower 2403

Dalleagles 747 Kirkconnel Sanquhar Mennock

waterside Mennock A702 Dalveen P Daer Resr

Dalmellington 987 Durisdeer

Alhang 2100 Scaur Sannchridge

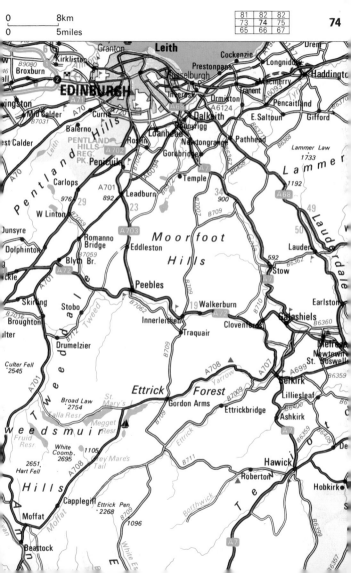

Burntisland

FIRTH

Inchkeith

North Berwick
Dirleton
Gullane
Aberlady
Whitekirk
Dren
Dunbar

Leith

Cockenzie
Longniddry
Linton

A198

Prestonpans
Musselburgh
Inveresk
Tranent
Haddington
Garvald
Ormiston
Pencaitland

Dalkeith
E. Saltoun
Gifford

Loanhead
Roslin
Bonnyrigg
Newtongrange
Pathhead
Gorebridge

Temple

Lammer Law
1733

L a m m e r m u i r   H i l l s

Longformacus

Leadburn

900

1192

Westruther
Du

Eddleston

Lauder

L a u d e r d a l e

A6105

M o o r f o o t
H i l l s

592

Stow

Greenlaw
Ga

Peebles

Gordon
Eccles
Birg

Walkerburn
19
Earlston
Nenthorn
Ednam

Innerleithen
Galashiels
Clovenfords
Smailholm
Kelso

Traquair
Melrose
Newtown
St. Boswells
Maxton
Heiton

E t t r i c k   F o r e s t
A708
Yarrow
Selkirk
18
A699

Gordon Arms
Lilliesleaf
Crailing
Eckford

Ettrickbridge
Ashkirk
T e v i o t d a l e
Jedburgh

A7
Denholm

Hawick

Roberton
Bonchester Br.
Camptown
Hobkirk

Southdean
Carter Bar

spath
A1107   B6438
St. Abb's Hd.
St. Abb's
ntshouse
Coldingham   Eyemouth
Ayton   Burnmouth
B6355
Chirnside
B6355
Whiteadder   A6105

**Berwick-
upon-Tweed**
B6460   ▲
Spittal
B6461   A1167
36437
Norham   A1

Ancroft   Beal
B6354
Duddo   Holy Island

Cornhill
on Tweed   Etal   B6353
Ford   Lowick   Budle Bay

Farne Islands

Wark
B6352
B6351   Belford   ▲
B6342   Bamburgh
Doddington   Seahouses

Kirknewton   North
etholm   Sunderland   Beadnell
B6349   B1340
Wooler   Chatton   B6348   Warenford   Beadnell Bay
A697
Chillingham   B6347   Embleton
▲

The Cheviot   Eglingham   ▲
. 2676   B6347
B6346

Ingram   Longhoughton
Breamish   Aln

Whittingham   Alnwick   Lesbury
B6341   A1   Alnmouth

Alwinton   Edlingham

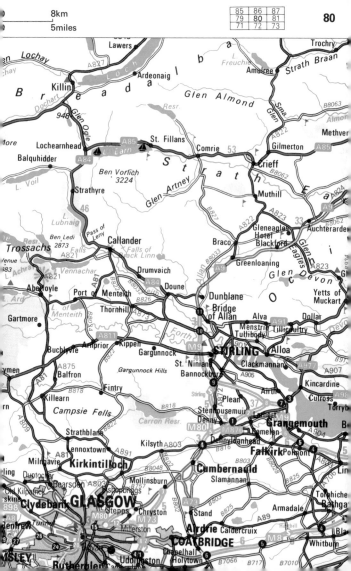

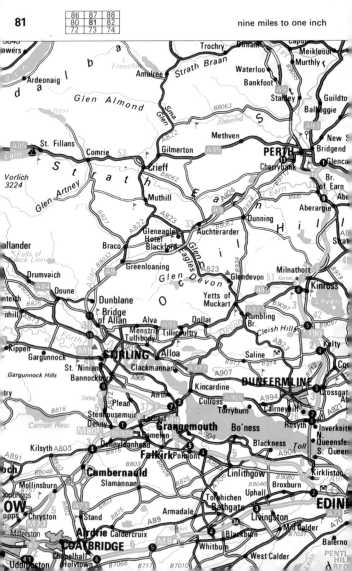

8km
5miles

Todhills

Muirhead

DUNDEE

ngforgan

Gowrie

Newport-on-Tay

Wormit

Toll

Kilmany

Balmullo

Dairsie

Cupar

Ceres

Pitscottie

Ladybank

Fife

Kettlebridge

Markinch

Largo

Leven

Buckhaven

Wemyss

Dysart

KIRKCALDY

Kinghorn

ntisland

Inchkeith

Muirdrum

Barry

Carnoustie

Monifieth

Broughty Ferry

Tayport

Firth of Tay

Leuchars

St. Andrews

Eden

Kingsbarns

Largo Ward

Colinsburgh

Kilconquhar

Elie

Crail

Kilrenny

Anstruther

Pittenweem

St. Monans

I. of May

FIRTH OF FORTH

Fidra

Bass Rock

North Berwick

Dirleton

Gullane

Aberlady

Whitekirk

Dunbar

Leith

Cockenzie

Prestonpans

Mosselburgh

Macmerry

Tranent

Pencaitland

Haddington

Drem

Linton

Garvald

Ormiston

E. Saltoun

Gifford

Dalkeith

Newtongrange

Pathhead

Loanhead

Lammer Law

Hills

Abbe

Todhills

Arbroath

Muirhead

Bell

Toll

Wormit

Ceres

Largo

Leven

Bass Rock

Longniddry

Garvald

Inveresk

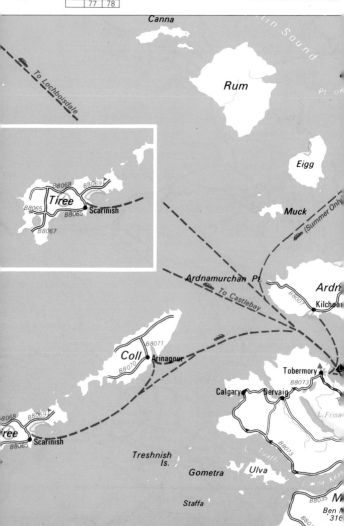

Canna

Sea of the Hebrides

Rum

To Lochboisdale

Pt. of

Eigg

B8068 B8069

Tiree

B8065
B8065 Scarinish

Muck

(Summer Only)

B8067

Ardnamurchan Pt.

Ardn

B8007 Kilchoan

To Castlebay

B8071

Coll

B8070 Arinagour

Tobermory

Calgary Dervaig

B8073

B8068 B8069

L. Frisa

ree B8065 Scarinish

*Treshnish
Is.*

L. Tuath

B8073

Gometra *Ulva*

Lona Keal

B8035 *M*

Ben M

Staffa 316

B8073

8km
5miles

Teangue

Airor

KNOYDART

Kinloch
Hourn

Glen
Glen

L. Clua

L. Lo

(Summer
Only)

Mallaig

Morar

L. Quoich

Murlaggan

B8005

L. Arkaig

L Nevis

A830

Arisaig

Loch Morar

Gair

L nan Uamh

L Eilt

47

Glenfinnan

B8044

of Arisaig

Lochailort

A861

MOIDART

Loch Shiel

A830

A861 *Loch Eil*

Corpach

Loch

Fort
William

Kinlochmoidart

Acharacle

Salen

B8007

A861

Polloch

Corran

Loch Linnhe

L

L Sunart

A884

Strontian

Inversanda

A861

N.Ballachulish

Onich

Le

ulin

M o r v e r n

B8043

Kentallen
Ballachulish

Glencoe

Gle

A828

·37

Appin

Claggan

A884

L o c h   L i n n h e

49

Bidean
nam
Bian

Glen

Lochaline

Portnacroish

Port
Appin

L MU

Barcaldine

Ben Star
3541

849

shnish

Craignure

A849

L i s m o r e

L Creran

A828

B345

Loch

Etive

Lochdonhead

Connel

A85

Oban

Bonawe

Taynuilt

Ben Cruachan
3689

Pass

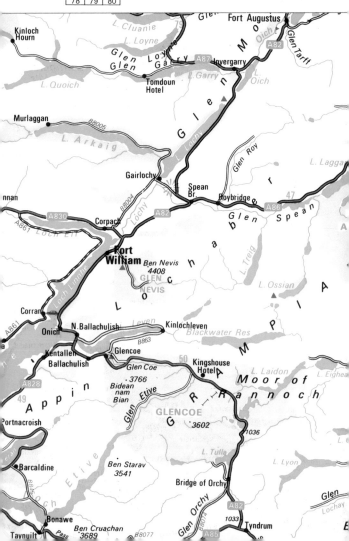

Kinloch Hourn

L. Cluanie

L. Loyne

Glen Loyne

Glen Garry

Fort Augustus

Oich

Glen Tarff

A82

Invergarry

A87

Tomdoun Hotel

L. Garry

L. Oich

Glen

Murlaggan

B8005

L. Arkaig

L. Lochy

Glen Roy

L. Laggan

Gairlochy

Spean Br.

Roybridge

A86

47

Glen Spean

R

nnan

A830

A861

B8004

Lochy

A82

Corpach

Loch Eil

Glen

Spean

A

Fort William

Ben Nevis 4408

GLEN NEVIS

Loch Linnhe

a

c

h

L. Treig

b

L. Ossian

M

P

I

A

Corran

Onich

N.Ballachulish

Leven

Kinlochleven

Blackwater Res

A861

Kentallen

Ballachulish

Glencoe

B863

Glen Coe

Kingshouse Hotel

50

L. Laidon

Moor of

L. Eighea

A828

49

Appin

Bidean nam Bian

3766

Etive

GLENCOE

G

R

3602

1036

R

Rannoch

L. Lyon

Portnacroish

Glen

Ben Starav 3541

L. Tulla

Bridge of Orchy

Barcaldine

Etive

Loch

Bonawe

Taynuilt

Ben Cruachan 3689

Pass

B8077

Glen Orchy

A82

1033

Tyndrum

A85

Glen

Lochay

E

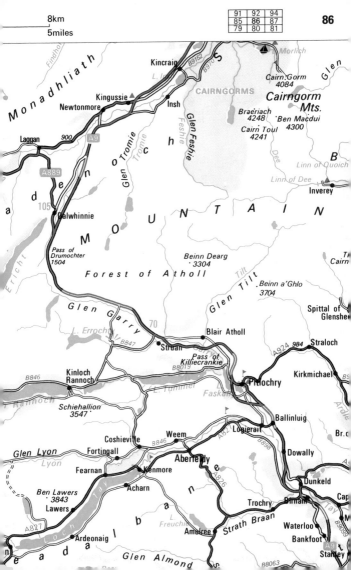

8km
5miles

Monadhliath

Findhorn

Morlich

Kincraig B9152 B9170

L. In h

Kingussie

Newtonmore

Insh

CAIRNGORMS

Cairn Gorm
4084

Glen

Cairngorm
Mts.

Braeriach
4248

Ben Macdui
4300

Cairn Toul
4241

Laggan

900

A9

Glen Tromie

Glen Feshie

Dee

B

Linn of Quoich

A889

Tromie

Glen

Linn of Dee

Inverey

a

d

e

n

105

Dalwhinnie

M

O

U

N

T

A

I

N

Ericht

Pass of
Drumochter
1504

Beinn Dearg
3304

T

Cairn

Forest of Atholl

Tilt

Beinn a'Ghlo
3704

Glen Tilt

Glen Garry

70

Spittal of
Glenshee

L. Errochd

B847

Blair Atholl

A924

984

Straloch

Struan

Pass of
Killiecrankie

Kirkmichael

B8

B846

Kinloch
Rannoch

B8019

Pitlochry

Rannoch

Schiehallion
3547

L. Tummel

Faskall

Ballinluig

Ardle

Br. o

Glen Lyon

Coshieville

Weem

Logierait

Dowally

Lyon

Fortingall

B846

A827

B898

Fearnan

Kenmore

Aberfeldy

A826

Dunkeld

Ben Lawers
3843

Acharn

B

Trochry

Birnam

Cap

Lawers

A827

Loch Tay

a

n

e

L
Freuchi

Strath Braan

Waterloo

Bankfoot

n

Ardeonaig

Glen Almond

Amulree

A9

Stanley

e

a

d

a

b

a

s

B8063

M

Morlich

Glen Avon

Cairn Gorm 4084

Morven 2862

IGORMS

Cairngorm Mts.

Ben Avon 3843

Gairn

Br. of Gairn

A939

A93

Ballater

B976

Braeriach 4248

Ben Macdui 4300

Cairn Toul 4241

B

Braemar

r

a

e

m

a

r

Glen Muick

Glen Tan

Linn of Quoich

Linn of Dee

Inverey

Dee

Lochnagar 3786

L. Muick

Mt. Ke 3077

A

I

N

S

Glen Clunie

L. Lee

g

Tilt

The Cairnwell 3059

2199

Glas Maol 3502

M

Beinn a'Ghlo 3704

A93

Glen Clova

Clova

B955

en Tilt

Spittal of Glenshee

Glen Isla

Glen Prosen

Atholl

A924   984

Straloch

Shee

Glenshee

B951

Glenisla

Backwater Resr.

Dykehead

B955

m

B957

Pitlochry

Kirkmichael

B950

Isla

B951

Kirriemuir

h

Lair

51

A926

A928

A926

A

Ballinluig

Ardle

A924

Br. of Cally

A93

Alyth

Craigton

Dean

Glamis

Logierait

B898

Dowally

A926

Blairgowrie

Ruthven

A928

14

Trochry

Dunkeld

Rattray

B947

a

A923

Meigle

Newtyle

Todhills

Birnam

Caputh

Meikleour

Coupar Angus

30

Hills

Strath Braan

Waterloo

Bankfoot

Murthly

Tay

B9099

A94

Burrelton

B994

Muirhead

A9

Stanley

Guildtown

B953

A923

DUNDEE

B8063

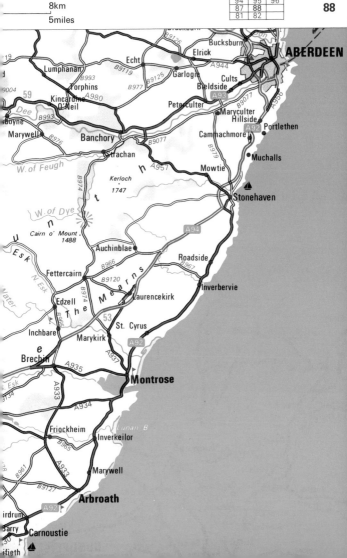

8km
5miles

Brackburn
Bucksburn
Echt
Elrick
ABERDEEN
Lumphanan
B9126
B9119
Garlogie
Cults
A944
Torphins
B993
B977
Bieldside
B9125
Kincardine
O'Neil
A980
Peterculter
A93
B9077
B956
9004
59
Dee
B993
Maryculter
Hillside
A92
Portlethen
Boyne
B976
Marywell
Banchory
Cammachmore
B9077
Muchalls
Strachan
h
B979
t
A957
Mowtie
Kerloch
1747
W. of Feugh
n
Stonehaven
W. of Dye
u
A94
Cairn o' Mount.
1488
Auchinblae
Roadside
E
s
k
M
B966
B967
N Esk
Fettercairn
B9120
e
a
r
Inverbervie
Water
B974
n
s
Edzell
T
Laurencekirk
h
B966
53
e
St. Cyrus
Inchbare
A92
Marykirk
e
Brechin
A935
A937
Esk
A933
Montrose
B734
A934
Friockheim
Lunan B
B965
Inverkeilor
B961
A933
Marywell
B9127
Arbroath
A92
irdrum
Barry
Carnoustie
ifieth

Rubha Hunish

Score B

Kilmaluag

A855

rtain

Vaternish Pt.

Staffin

Uig

Geary

Loch
Snizort

A855

Dunvegan Hd.

Stein

B886

A850

The Storr
2360

Kensaleyre

Milovaig

B884

Dunvegan

Edinbane

Bernisdale

Carbost

Roskhill

B885

Portree

Macleod's
Tables

A850

Bracadale

S k y e

B885

L Bracadale

Fiskavaig

B8009

Drynoch

A863

S

Carbost

Sligachan
Hotel

A85

SEA

OF THE

Cuillin
Hills
3257

Bla
30

Glenbrittle

Sgurr
Alasdair

L
Coru

BRIDES

L Brittle

B8

Soay

L. Scavaig

Elg

Canna

Cuillin Sound

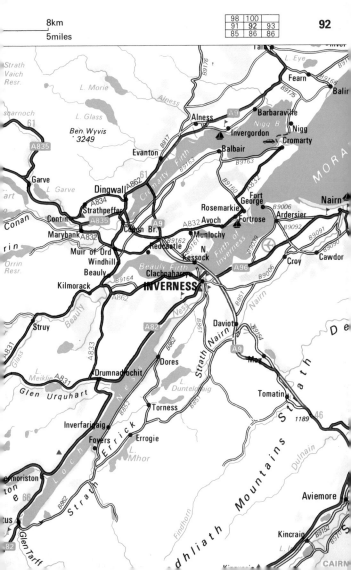

8km
5miles

Strath
Vaich
Resr.

L. Morie

Alness

Tain

L. Eye

Fearn

B9176

B9166

Balir

B9175

Barbaraville

A9

Nigg

Cromarty

Strath Glass

Ben Wyvis
3249

L. Glass

sqarnoch

61

A835

Garve

L Garve

Evanton

Balbair

Invergordon

Nigg B.

MORA

B817

Cromarty Firth

Dingwall

A862

Strathpeffer

61

B9163

B9163

Fort
George

Rosemarkie

B9006

Nairn

A834

A835

Contin

Conan

Marybank

A832

Cononr Br.

A9

A832 Avoch

Fortrose

Ardersier

B9092

B9091

B9006

art

L Garve

rin

Muir of Ord

Redcastle

Munlochy

B9161

N.
Kessock

Firth of
Inverness

Croy

Cawdor

B9090

Orrin
Resr.

Windhill

Beauly

B9164

Clachnaharry

Beauly Firth

A96

B9006

Kilmorack

A862

INVERNESS

B851

Nairn

Struy

Beauly

A82

Daviot

Strath Nairn

A9

Mol

De

Glass

A831

A833

L.
Meiklie A831

Drumnadrochit

Dores

B862

B861

Tomatin

1189

46

Glen Urquhart

Loch Ness

Torness

B862

L.
Duntelchaig

Strath

Inverfarigaig

Foyers

Errogie

Errick

L.
Mhor

Dulnain

Strath

emoriston
ton
e 66

B862

Glen Tarff

ffus

A82

Aviemore

dhliath Mountains

Findhorn

Kincraig

B9152

CAIRN

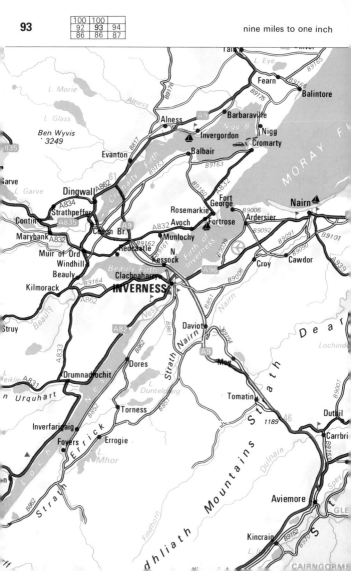

Tain

L Eye

Fearn

Balintore

L Morie

L Glass

Ben Wyvis
·3249

Alness

B9176

A9

Barbaraville

Invergordon

Nigg B

Nigg

Cromarty

MORAY F

Evanton

B817

Balbair

B9163

Garve

L Garve

Dingwall

A862

Cromarty Firth

B9163

B9160

A835

Contin

A834

Strathpeffer

A835

Fort
George

Rosemarkie

B9006

Nairn

Marybank

A832

Cleign Br.

A9

Avoch

A832

Fortrose

Ardersier

B9092

B9091

B9101

Muir of Ord

Munlochy

B9161

N

Firth
of
Inverness

B9039

Croy

Cawdor

A939

Windhill

Neudcastle

Kessock

A96

B9006

Beauly

Clachnaharry

Kilmorack

B9164

INVERNESS

A862

B851

Nairn

Struy

A833

Ness

Daviot

B9154

Beauly

Dear

Leiklie

A831

L

Drumnadrochit

B862

Dores

Strath Nairn

Duntelchaig

A9

Moy

Lochind

n Urquhart

Tomatin

B9007

Torness

B851

Dulnain

Duthil

1189

46

Carrbri

B9154

Inverfarigaig

Errogie

Strath

Fovers

L
Mhor

Errick

Findhorn

Spey

GLE

dhliath Mountains

Aviemore

Loch

Strath

B862

Kincraig

B9152

B9152

S

CAIRNGORMS

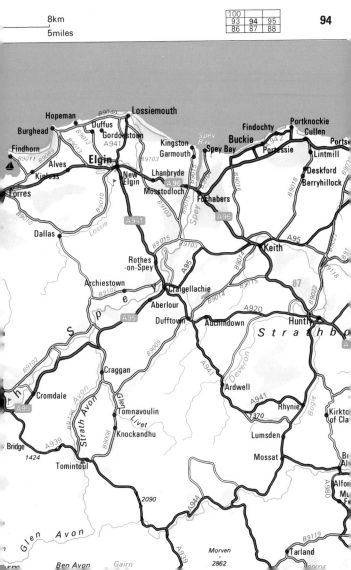

8km
5miles

Hopeman   **Lossiemouth**   B9040
Burghead   Duffus
B9012   Gordonstoun
Findochty   **Portknockie**
Cullen
Buckie   Ports
Findhorn   A941   Spey Bay   Portessie   Lintmill
B9011   Kingston   Garmouth   Spey Bay   Deskford
Alves   **Elgin**   B9103   Berryhillock
Kinloss   New   Lhanbryde   A96   B9018   B9017
Forres   Elgin   Mosstodloch   Fochabers
B9010   A96
Dallas   Lossie   B9015   A95   A95
Rothes   -on-Spey   67   B9118
Archiestown   B9102   Keith   B9022
S   p   e   y   Craigellachie   B9014   B9115
Aberlour   A920   **Hunt**
A95   Dufftown   Auchindown   **Strathbo**
S   h   Craggan   Avon   Deveron   A
Cromdale   Glen   Ardwell
A95   Livet   Tomnavoulin   A941   Rhynie   Kirkto
Bridge   1424   Knockandhu   Lumsden   of Cla
Tomintoul   Mossat   Br
Al
2090   Alfor
A944   Mu
A980
Glen   Avon   B9119
Ben Avon   Gairn   Morven   **Tarland**
2862   B9004
B9009
B9008
A939
A939

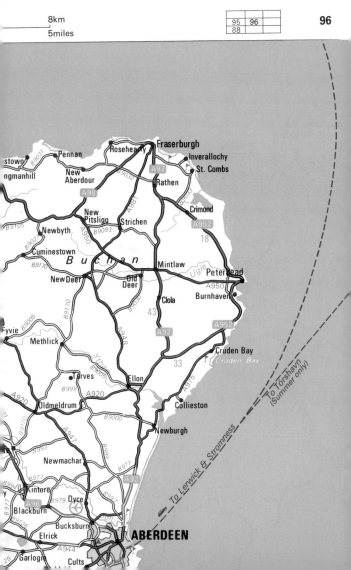

Fraserburgh
Inverallochy
Roseheaty
Pennan
St. Combs
stown
ngmanhill
New
Aberdour
Rathen
A92
B9031
B9032
A98
Crimond
New
Pitsligo
Strichen
A952
Newbyth
B9105
B9093
18
Newbyth
A950
A98
Cuminestown
B9170
Buchan
Mintlaw
Ugie
Peterhead
NewDeer
Old
Deer
A950
B9030
Clola
Burnhaven
B9170
43
A952
Fyvie
B9005
A948
A92
Methlick
Cruden Bay
Cruden Bay
Ythan
B9005
33
Tarves
Ellon
A975
B999
A920
A920
Oldmeldrum
B9000
Collieston
A947
Newburgh
B9993
Newmachar
B977
A92
B999
Kintore
B979
Dyce
A975
A96
Blackburn
B9125
B977
Bucksburn
Elrick
ABERDEEN
Garlogie
A944
Cults

To Torshavn
(Summer only)

To Lerwick & Stromness

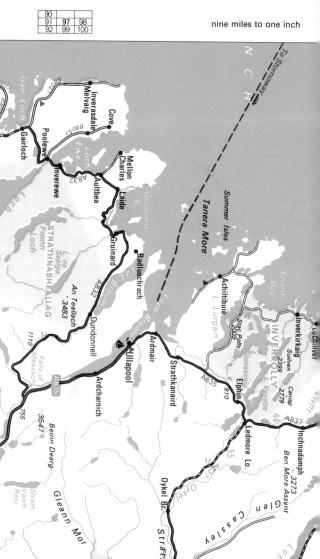

8km
5miles

Pt. of Stoer

Culkein

Drumbeg

Eddrachillis
Bay

Handa

Scourie

Badcall

Kylesku

Kylestrome

A894

Laxford Br.

Ben Stack
2364

Arkle
2580

Rhiconich
Foinaven

2890

Kinlochbervie

Cape Wrath

The Parbh

Kyle of Durness

Durness

Smoo

A838

Dionard

Reay
Forest

L. More

L. Stack

L. Eriboll

Eribol

A838

63

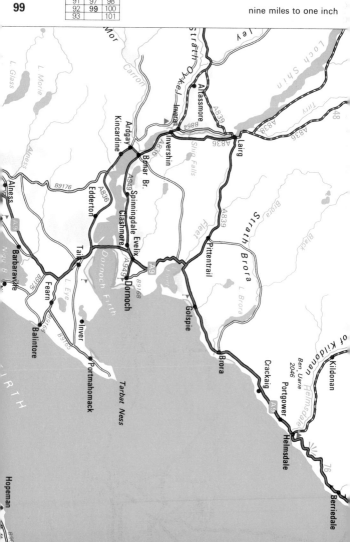

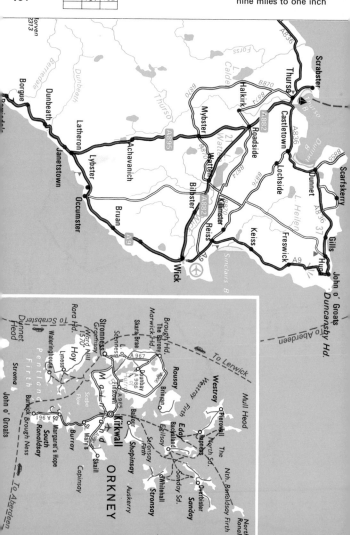

0   8km
0   5miles

To Lerwick

Rora Hd.
Brough Hd.
Marwick Hd.
Yesnaby
B9056
Twatt
Birsay
A966
A967
Stromness
A965
L. of Stenness
A967
A966
B9057
Swann
Eynhallow
Wasbister
Ward Hill 1565
Rackwick
Hoy
B9047
Lyness
Graemsay
Ward Hill
Orphir
A965
Dounby
Finstown
Woodwick
A966
Evie
B9064
Rousay
Tor Ness
Fara
Flotta
Cava
Scapa Flow
A964
Kirkwall
B. of Firth
Wyre
Egilsay
Binion
Eday
Walls
Cantick Hd.
Sd. of Hoxa
A961
St. Margaret's Hope
Grim Ness
St. Mary's
A960
A961
Gairsay
Linga Holm
Eday Sound
Backaland
Swona
A961
S. Ronaldsay
Burray
Rose Ness
A960
B9059
Balfour
B9058
Rerwick Hd.
Shapinsay
B9063
Whitehall
Old Head
Burwick
Deer Sd.
B9051
Shapinsay Sound
Mull Hd.
Lamb Hd.
Stronsay
B9060
Papa Stronsay
Sanday Sound
Pt. of Ayre
Skaill
Copinsay
Auskerry Sd.
Auskerry
B9061
Stronsay Firth
Lerwick
Pentland Firth

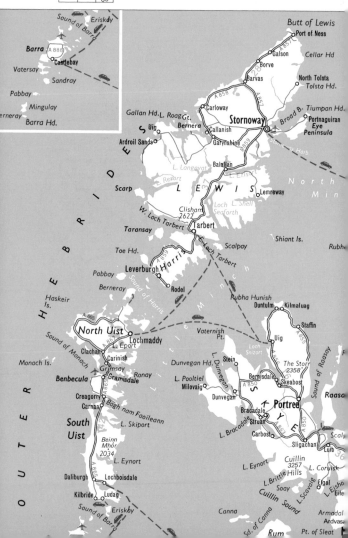

Sound of Barra
Eriskay
Barra A 888
Castlebay
Vatersay
Sandray
Pabbay
Mingulay
erneray
Barra Hd.

Butt of Lewis
Port of Ness
A 857
Galson
Borve
Cellar Hd.
Barvas
North Tolsta
Tolsta Hd.
A 858
Carloway
A 857
Gallan Hd. L. Roag Gt.
Stornoway
Broad B. Tiumpan Hd.
S Uig
Bernera
Callanish
Portnaguiran
Eye
Peninsula
Ardroil Sands
Garynahine
Stornoway Harb.
A 859
Balallan
L. Erisort
North
Min
L. Langavat
L E W I S
Resort
Lemreway
Scarp
Loch L. Shell
Seaforth
W. Loch Tarbert
Clisham
2622
Tarbert
E. Loch Tarbert
Shiant Is.
Rubhe
Taransay
Scalpay
Toe Hd.
Harris
A 859
Pabbay
Leverburgh
Berneray
Rodel
Sound of Harris
Rubha Hunish
Duntulm
Kilmaluag
Haskeir
Is.
A 865
North Uist
Lochmaddy
Vaternish
Pt.
Uig
A 855
Staffin
Clachan
L. Eport
Carinish
Dunvegan Hd.
Stein
Loch
Snizort
The Storr
2358
Monach Is.
Grimsay
Ronay
Bernisdale
A 850
Skeabost
Raasa
Benbecula
Gramisdale
L. Pooltiel
Milovaig
Dunvegan
Portree
Creagorry
Bagh nam Faoileann
Bracadale
Struan
S K Y E
A 850
Carnan
Carbost
A 863
**South
Uist**
L. Skiport
Beinn
Mhór
2034
L. Bracadale
Sligachan
Lurb
36
L. Eynort
Cuillin
3257
Hills
L. Coruisk
Daliburgh
Lochboisdale
L. Eynort
L. Brittle
Soay
L. Scavaig
Egol
Eije
Kilbride
Ludag
Cuillin Sound
Armadal
Ardvasa
Eriskay
Sound of Barra
Canna
Rum
Pt. of Sleat
O U T E R
H E B R I D E S
Sound of Monach

0 30km
0 20miles

Muckle Flugga
Burra Firth
Herma Ness
Norwick
Haroldswick
Baltasound   Balta
A 968 **Unst**
Cullivoe   Uyeasound
Dalsetter   Belmont
Gutcher Uyea
Isbister   Mid Yell   **Fetlar** Funzie
South-haa   **Yell**
W.   Colgrave Sd.
The Faither   Sandwick Otterswick
North Collafirth   Ollaberry   Burravoe
Esha Ness   Hillswick   Heoga Ness
Stenness   A 970   Mossbank
St Magnus   Scatsta   Out
Bay   A 968   Skerries
Muckle Roe   Brae   Lunna
A 360   Laxo
Voe   Dury Voe   Whalsay
Papa Stour   Aith   **SHETLAND**
Sandness   M a i n l a n d   A 971
Walls Tresta
Vaila   Reawick
Lerwick
Ham **Foula**   I. of Noss
Scalloway   **Bressay**   To Bergen & Hanstolm
Hamnavoe   Bressay Sd.   (Summer Only)
West Burra   Cunningsburgh
Cliff Sd.   Sandwick
To Tórshavn & Seydhisfjordhur   Mousa
(Summer Only)   Scousburgh
Fitful Head   A 970
Tolob   **Sumburgh Head**
Sumburgh

To Stromness   Stonybreck **Fair Isle**   To Aberdeen

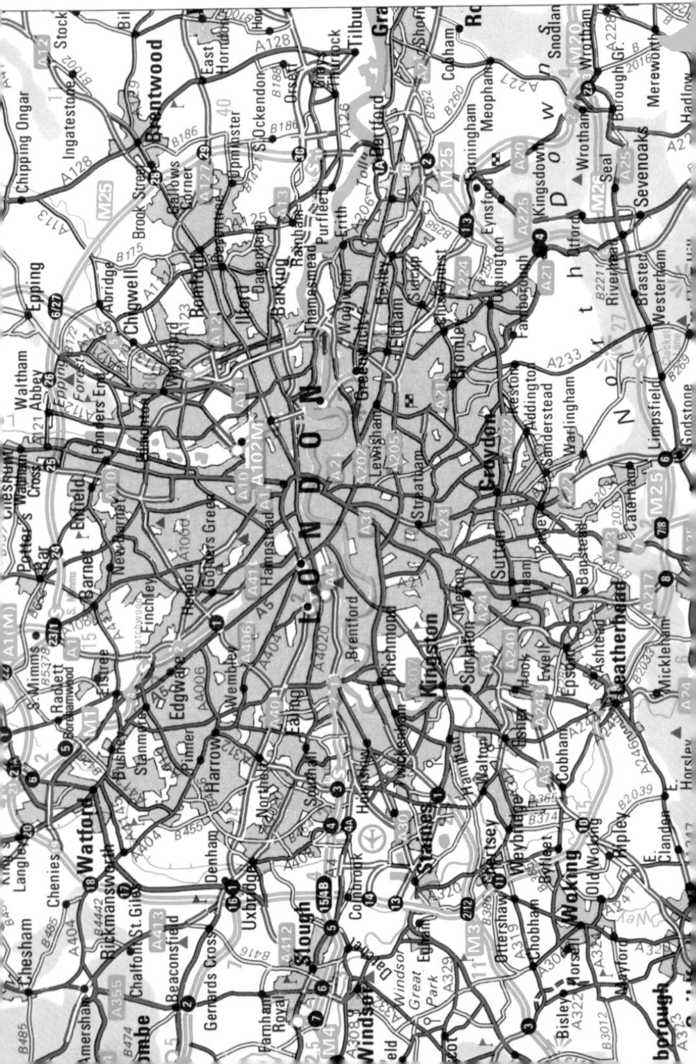

Index

This index comprises a selection of names and locations of towns and villages based on population, route importance, and postal significance.

The reference number refers to the page, and the letter refers to the section of the map in which the index entry can be found, as divided into **a**, **b**, **c**, and **d** thus:

A

Abbey St.Bathans	75b	Adderbury	29c
Abbey Town	65d	Addington	19d
Abbotsbury	8c	Adwick-le-Street	48a
Aberaeron	25a	Ainsdale	51d
Aberargie	81b	Aintree	45b
Abercarn	24d	Aird of Sleat	84a
Aberchirder	95b	Airdrie	73b
Aberdare	24a	Airth	81c
Aberdaron	43c	Albrighton	35d
Aberdeen	96c	Alcester	28a
Aberdour	81d	Aldbrough	56c
Aberdyfi	33c	Aldeburgh	41d
Aberedw	26a	Alderley Edge	46b
Aberfeldy	86d	Alderminster	28b
Aberffraw	43b	Aldershot	11a
Abergavenny	24b	Alexandria	79d
Abergele	44b	Alford (Grampian)	95d
Abergwynfi	24a	Alford (Lincs)	50c
Aberlady	82c	Alfreton	48c
Aberllefenni	33b	Alfriston	12c
Aberlour	94a	Alkham	14a
Abernethy	81b	Allanby	65d
Aberporth	22a	Allenheads	67d
Abersoch	43d	Allesley	28b
Abertillery	24b	Allgreave	47c
Aberystwyth	25b	Alloa	80d
Abingdon	17b	Almondsbury	15b
Abington	73d	Alness	93a
Aboyne	88a	Alnmouth	68a
Accrington	52c	Alnwick	68a
Acharacle	84c	Alpheton	32a
Acharn	86c	Alresford	10a
Achavanich	101a	Alrewas	36a
Achiltibuie	97b	Alston	66d
Achintree	90b	Alston Cross	28c
Achnasheen	91b	Altassmore	99b
Acklington	68a	Altnaharra	100a
Acock's Green	36c	Alton	10b
Acomb	54b	Altrincham	46b
Acton Turville	16a	Alva	81c

a | b
c | d

Alvanley	46c	Arundel	11c
Alvaston	36b	Ascot	18c
Alvechurch	28a	Asfordby	37b
Alyth	87d	Ash	14a
Amble	68a	Ashbourne	36a
Ambleside	58c	Ashburton	4a
Amersham	18a	Ashby	49b
Amesbury	9b	Ashby de la Zouch	36b
Amlwch	43b	Ashford (Kent)	13b
Ammanford	23b	Ashington	68a
Ampleforth	61d	Ashstead	19c
Ampthill	30c	Ashton Keynes	16b
Amulree	80b	Ashton-under-Lyne	47a
Ancaster	38a	Ashton-in-Makerfield	46a
Ancroft	76c	Askham	57d
Andover	9b	Aspatria	65d
Andoversford	28c	Aston	48a
Annan	65d	Atherstone	36d
Annbank	72c	Atherton	46a
Anstruther	82b	Attleborough	42a
Appleby	58b	Atwick	56a
Applecross	90a	Atworth	16c
Appledore (Devon)	5b	Auchencairn	64d
Appledore (Kent)	13d	Auchentiber	72a
Arbroath	88c	Auchinblae	88a
Archiestown	94a	Auchindown	95a
Ardarroch	90c	Auchinleck	73c
Ardbeg	69b	Auchterarder	81b
Ardcharnich	97c	Auchtermuchty	82a
Ardentinny	79d	Aultbea	97a
Ardeonaig	80a	Aviemore	93d
Ardersier	93b	Avoch	93a
Ardfern	78a	Avonmouth	15b
Ardgay	99c	Axbridge	15c
Ardlui	79b	Axminster	7d
Ardlussa	77d	Aylesbury	30c
Ardmair	97b	Aylesham	14a
Ardminish	70a	Aylsham	40a
Ardrishaig	78c	Aynho	29d
Ardrossan	71b	Ayr	71d
Ardtalla	69b	Aysgarth	59d
Arduaine	78a	Ayton	76a
Arinagour	83c		
Arisaig	84a	**B**	
Armadale (Skye)	84a		
Armadale (Highland)	100b	Backaland	101d
Arncliffe	52b	Bacup	52d
Arnesby	37c	Badcall	98c
Arnisdale	90d	Badluachrach	97a
Arnprior	80c	Bagby	61d
Arnside	51b	Bagshot	18c
Arrochar	79d	Bakewell	47d
Arthog	33a	Bala	44d

Balallan	103b	Basingstoke	17d
Balbair	93a	Baslow	47d
Balbeggie	81b	Bath	15d
Balcombe	12a	Bathgate	73b
Baldock	30d	Batley	54c
Balerno	74a	Battle	13c
Balfour	101c	Battlefield	35a
Balintore	93b	Baumber	50c
Ballachulish	85c	Bawtry	48b
Ballantrae	63a	Baynards Green	29d
Ballater	87b	Beaconsfield	18a
Ballaugh	51c	Beadnell	76d
Ballinluig	86d	Beal	76c
Ballygrant	69b	Beaminster	8c
Balmaha	79d	Beattock	65b
Balmullo	82a	Beaulieu	9d
Balsham	31b	Beauly	92a
Baltasound	104b	Beaumaris	44a
Bamber Bridge	52c	Bebington	45b
Bamburgh	76d	Beccles	42c
Bampton	7a	Beckingham	49a
Banbury	29c	Bedale	60c
Banchory	28a	Bedford	30b
Banff	95b	Bedlington	68c
Bangor	44a	Bedworth	36d
Bannockburn	81c	Beer	7d
Banstead	19c	Beeston	37a
Barbaraville	93b	Beith	71b
Barcaldine	79a	Belford	76d
Bardon Mill	67d	Bellingham	67b
Bardsea	51b	Bellochantuy	70c
Bargoed	24b	Bellshill	73a
Bargrennan	63b	Belmont	52c
Barking	19b	Belper	48c
Barlborough	48b	Belsay	68a
Barmouth	33a	Bembridge	10c
Barnard Castle	60a	Benson	17b
Barnet	19a	Bentley	48a
Barnoldswick	53a	Bere Regis	8d
Barnsley	48a	Berkeley	15b
Barnstaple	6a	Berkhamsted	18a
Barr	63b	Bernisdale	89b
Barrhead	72a	Berriedale	99b
Barrhill	63b	Berryhillock	95b
Barrow	56c	Berwick-upon-Tweed	76a
Barrow-in-Furness	51a	Bethesda	44a
Barry	24d	Bettyhill	100b
Barton (Humberside)	56c	Betws-y-Coed	44b
Barton (Bedfordshire)	30c	Beulah	26a
Barton Mills	31b	Beverley	56c
Barvas	103b	Bewdley	27b
Baschurch	34b	Bexhill-on-Sea	13d
Basildon	20a	Bexley	19b

Bicester	29d	Blagdon (Somerset)	7b
Bickley Moss	46c	Blair Atholl	86d
Biddendon	13d	Blairgowrie	87c
Biddulph	47c	Blakeney (Norfolk)	40a
Bideford	5b	Blakeney (Glos)	15b
Bidford	28a	Blakenham	32b
Bigbury on Sea	3d	Blanchland	67d
Biggar	74c	Blandford Forum	8b
Biggleswade	30b	Blankney	49d
Bilbister	101b	Blantyre	73a
Billericay	20a	Blaydon	68c
Billesdon	37d	Blean	14a
Billingborough	38a	Bletchingley	12a
Billingshurst	11b	Blewbury	17b
Bilston	35d	Blindley Heath	12a
Bingham	37b	Blofield	42c
Bingley	53d	Bloxwich	36c
Binley	29a	Blubberhouses	53b
Birchington	14b	Blyth (Northumberland)	68a
Birdlip	28c	Blyth Bridge	74a
Birgham	75d	Blythburgh	41d
Birkenhead	45b	Blyton	49a
Birmingham	36c	Boat of Garton	93d
Birnam	87c	Bodfari	45c
Birsay	101d	Bodmin	2b
Birtley	68c	Bognor Regis	11c
Bishop Auckland	60a	Boldon	68d
Bishopbriggs	73a	Boldre	9d
Bishop Burton	55d	Bollington	47a
Bishops Castle	34c	Bolton	46a
Bishop's Caundle	8a	Bolventor	2b
Bishop's Cleeve	28c	Bonar Bridge	99a
Bishops Lydeard	7b	Boncath	22a
Bishop's Stortford	31c	Bonchester Bridge	75d
Bishops Waltham	10a	Bo'ness	81d
Bisley	18c	Bonhill	79d
Bitterne	10a	Bonnyrigg	74b
Blaby	37c	Boothby Pagnell	38a
Blackbrook	35b	Bootle (Cumbria)	57d
Blackburn	52c	Bootle (Merseyside)	45b
Blackford	81a	Boreland	65b
Blackmoor Gate	6a	Borough Green	20c
Blackness	81d	Boroughbridge	54a
Blackpool	51d	Borrowdale	57b
Blackwaterfoot	70c	Borth	33c
Blackwood (S'clyde)	73b	Borve	103b
Blackwood (Gwent)	24d	Boscastle	5c
Bladnoch	64c	Bosley	47c
Blaenau Ffestiniog	44c	Boston	50c
Blaenavon	24b	Botesdale	41b
Blaenporth	22a	Bothwell	73a
Blaenrhondda	24a	Botley (Oxon)	17b
Blagdon (Avon)	15d	Botley (Hants)	10a

Bourne	38a	Bridge of Weir	71b
Bournemouth	9c	Bridgend (Strathclyde)	69a
Bovey Tracey	4a	Bridgend (Mid Glamorgan)	24c
Bow	4a	Bridgnorth	35d
Bow Street	33c	Bridgwater	7b
Bowes	59b	Bridlington	56a
Bowland Bridge	58c	Bridport	8c
Bowling	80c	Brierley Hill	35d
Bowmore	69a	Brigg	49b
Bowness	58c	Brighouse	53d
Box	16c	Brighstone	10c
Bracadale	89d	Brightling	13c
Bracebridge	49d	Brightlingsea	32d
Brackley	29d	Brighton	12c
Bracknell	18c	Brinkley	31b
Braco	80b	Brinkworth	16a
Bradfield	17d	Brinyan	101d
Bradford	53d	Brisley	40a
Bradford-on-Avon	16c	Bristol	15b
Bradwell on Sea	20b	Briton Ferry	23d
Braemar	87a	Brixham	4c
Brailsford	36a	Brixworth	29b
Braintree	31d	Broad Chalke	9a
Bramdean	10a	Broad Clyst	7c
Bramham	54c	Broad Haven	21d
Bramley	11b	Broad Hinton	16b
Brampton (Cambs)	30b	Broadford	90c
Brampton (Cumbria)	66c	Broadstairs	14b
Brancaster	39b	Broadway	28d
Brancepeth	60a	Broadwey	8c
Brandesburton	56a	Broadwindsor	7d
Brandon (Durham)	60a	Brockenhurst	9d
Brandon (Suffolk)	39d	Brodick	70b
Branston	49d	Bromborough	45b
Brant Broughton	49d	Bromley	19d
Braunton	5b	Brompton	62d
Brayford	6a	Bromsgrove	28a
Breage	1d	Bromyard	27b
Breakish	90c	Bronnant	25b
Bream	15b	Brookland	13d
Brechin	88c	Brora	99b
Brecon	24a	Broseley	35c
Brede	13d	Brotton	62a
Bredhurst	20c	Brough	58b
Brentford	19a	Broughton (Borders)	74c
Brentwood	19b	Broughton (Cumbria)	57d
Brenzett	13d	Brownhills	36c
Bridge of Alford	95d	Broxburn	74a
Bridge of Allan	81c	Bruton	8a
Bridge of Cally	87c	Bryn-amman	25d
Bridge of Earn	81b	Bryn-crug	33c
Bridge of Gairn	87b	Bryneglwys	45c
Bridge of Orchy	85d	Brynmawr	24b

Bubwith	55d	Byrness	66b
Buckden	30b	Bythorne	30a
Buckfastleigh	4c		
Buckhaven	82c	**C**	
Buckie	94b		
Buckingham	29d	Cadbury	4a
Buckley	45d	Cadnam	9b
Bucks Green	11b	Caenby Corner	49b
Bucksburn	88b	Caerleon	15a
Bude	5c	Caernarfon	43b
Budleigh Salterton	7c	Caerphilly	24d
Builth Wells	26a	Caersws	34c
Bulwick	38c	Caerwent	15a
Bunessan	77a	Cairnbaan	78c
Bungay	42c	Cairnryan	63a
Bunny	37a	Caister-on-Sea	42d
Buntingford	31c	Caistor	49b
Bures	32c	Caldbeck	66c
Burford	28d	Caldecott	37d
Burgess Hill	12c	Calder Bridge	57c
Burgh le Marsh	50d	Caldercruix	72b
Burghead	94a	Caldicot	15b
Burley	53c	Caldwell	60a
Burnham	15c	Calgary	83d
Burnham Market	39b	Callander	80a
Burnham on Crouch	20b	Callanish	103b
Burnhaven	96b	Callington	3b
Burniston	62d	Calne	16c
Burnley	52d	Calveley	46c
Burnmouth	76a	Calver	47d
Burnopfield	68c	Camberley	18c
Burnsall	53b	Camborne	1d
Burntisland	82c	Cambridge	31a
Burravoe	104b	Camelford	5c
Burry Port	22d	Cammachmore	88b
Burscough Bridge	45b	Campbeltown	70c
Burslem	46d	Camptown	67a
Burton	49d	Cannich	92c
Burton Agnes	56a	Cannington	7b
Burton Leonard	54a	Cannock	35d
Burton in Kendal	58c	Canonbie	66a
Burton in Lonsdale	52a	Canterbury	14a
Burton upon Trent	36a	Canvey	20a
Burwash	13c	Capel	11b
Burwell (Cambs)	31b	Capenhurst	45d
Burwell (Lincs)	50a	Capplegill	74c
Burwick	101c	Caputh	87c
Bury	46b	Carbis Bay	1d
Bury St Edmonds	32a	Carbost	89b
Buttermere	57b	Cardiff	24d
Buttington	34a	Cardigan	22a
Buxton	47d	Carinish	103c
Byfleet	18d	Carisbrooke	10c

Carlisle	66c	Checkley	36a
Carlops	74a	Cheddar	15c
Carlton on Trent	48d	Chelmsford	20a
Carluke	73b	Cheltenham	28c
Carmarthen	22b	Chepstow	15b
Carnforth	51b	Cheriton	10a
Carno	33d	Chertsey	18d
Carnoustie	82b	Chesham	18b
Carnwath	73b	Cheshunt	19b
Carradale	70a	Chessell	10c
Carrbridge	93d	Chester	45d
Carrick Castle	78d	Chester-le-Street	68c
Carronbridge	65a	Chesterfield	48c
Carsphairn	64a	Chew Stoke	15d
Carstairs	73b	Chicheley	30a
Carter Bar	67a	Chichester	11c
Casterton	58c	Chicklade	9a
Castlebay	103a	Chiddingfold	11a
Castle Cary	98a	Chideock	7d
Castle Douglas	64d	Chigwell	19b
Castleford	54c	Chilham	14a
Castle Hedingham	32c	Chillingham	76c
Castle Kennedy	63d	Chilton Foliat	17c
Castle Rising	39b	Chinnor	18a
Castleside	68c	Chippenham	16a
Castleton (Derbys)	47b	Chipping Camden	28d
Castleton (N.Yorks)	62b	Chipping Norton	28d
Castletown	51c	Chipping Ongar	19b
Caterham	19a	Chipping Sodbury	15b
Catterick	60c	Chirnside	76a
Cavendish	32a	Chiseldon	16b
Cawdor	93b	Chiselhurst	19d
Caxton	31a	Chobham	18c
Cemaes Bay	43b	Chorley	52c
Ceres	82a	Christchurch	9d
Cerne Abbas	8c	Chryston	72b
Chagford	4a	Chudleigh	4a
Chale	10c	Chulmleigh	6c
Chalfont St. Giles	18d	Church Stretton	34d
Chandler's Ford	10a	Churchill	15c
Chapel Allerton	54c	Churston Ferrers	4c
Chapel en le Frith	47b	Cinderford	27d
Chapel St.Leonards	50d	Cirencester	16a
Chard	7b	Clachnaharry	92b
Charlbury	29c	Clackmannan	80d
Charlton Kings	28c	Clacton-on-Sea	32d
Charlwood	11b	Clanfield	10b
Charmouth	7d	Claonaig	70a
Chatham	20c	Clapham	52a
Chatteris	38d	Clarencefield	65d
Chatton	76c	Clashmore	99a
Cheadle (Staffs)	36a	Clashnessie	98a
Cheadle (Grtr Manchester)	46b	Clawton	5d

Clay Cross	48c	Connel	78a
Claydon	41a	Conon Bridge	92a
Clayton-le-Moors	52d	Consett	68c
Cleator	57a	Contin	92a
Cleehill	27b	Conwy	44a
Cleethorpes	50a	Conwyl Elfed	22a
Cleobury Mortimer	27b	Cooden	13c
Clevedon	15c	Cookham	18a
Cleveleys	51d	Coolham	11b
Clitheroe	52c	Coombe Bissett	9b
Cloughton	62d	Coombe Martin	6c
Clova	87b	Copplestone	6c
Clovelly	5b	Corbridge	67d
Clovenfords	75c	Corby	37d
Clun	34c	Corfe Castle	9c
Clydebank	72a	Corhampton	10a
Clynder	79d	Cornhill (Grampian)	95b
Clyst Honiton	7c	Cornhill on Tweed	76c
Coalville	36b	Cornwood	3d
Coatbridge	73a	Corpach	85a
Cobham (Surrey)	18d	Corran	84d
Cobham (Kent)	20c	Corrie Common	65b
Cockburnspath	75b	Corringham	49a
Cockenzie	82c	Corsham	16c
Cockermouth	57b	Corston	16a
Codicote	30d	Corwen	34a
Coggleshall	32c	Cosham	10a
Colchester	32c	Coshieville	86c
Cold Ashton	15d	Cotherstone	59b
Coldingham	76a	Cottenham	31a
Cold Norton	20a	Cottingham	56c
Coldstream	76c	Coupar Angus	87d
Coleford (Glos)	15b	Cove	79d
Coleshill	36c	Coventry	29a
Colintraive	78d	Coverack	2c
Collieston	96d	Cowbridge	24c
Collingham (W.Yorks)	54a	Cowdenbeath	81d
Collingham (Notts)	49c	Cowes	10c
Colmonell	63b	Cowfold	11b
Colnbrook	18b	Coxhoe	61a
Colne	52d	Coychurch	24c
Colpy	95d	Crackleybank	35b
Colsterworth	37b	Craigellachie	94b
Coltishall	42b	Craighouse	69b
Colwyn Bay	44b	Craignure	78a
Colyford	7d	Craigton	87d
Comrie	80b	Crail	82b
Congleton	46d	Cramlington	68c
Congresbury	15c	Cranborne	9a
Coningsby	50c	Cranbrook	13d
Conisbrough	48a	Cranford St.John	30a
Coniston	57d	Cranleigh	11b
Connah's Quay	45d	Cranswick	56a

Crathorne	61d
Craven Arms	34d
Crawford	73d
Crawfordjohn	73d
Crawley	11b
Cray	24a
Creagorry	103c
Credenhill	27c
Crediton	4a
Creetown	64c
Cresselly	21d
Crewe	46c
Crewkerne	7b
Crianlarich	79b
Cribyn	25a
Criccieth	43d
Crickhowell	26d
Cricklade	16b
Crieff	80b
Crinan	78c
Crockernwell	4a
Crockham Hill	12a
Croft	61c
Cromarty	93b
Cromdale	94c
Cromer	40b
Cromford	48a
Crook	60a
Crosby (Merseyside)	45b
Crosby (I.of W.)	51c
Crosby Ravensworth	58b
Croshills	53b
Cross Hands	23b
Cross-Keys	24d
Crossaig	70a
Crosshill	71d
Crowborough	12a
Crowcombe	7a
Crowland	38a
Crowle	55d
Crowthorne	18c
Croxton Kerrial	37b
Croydon	19d
Cruden Bay	96d
Crudgington	35a
Crudwell	16a
Crymmych	22a
Crynant	23b
Cuckfield	12a
Cudworth	48a
Culgaith	59a
Culkein	98a
Cullen	95b
Cullompton	7a
Culmstock	7a
Culross	81d
Cults	88b
Cumbernauld	73b
Cuminestown	96a
Cumnock	72c
Cunningsburgh	104d
Cupar	82a
Currie	74a
Cury Cross	1d
Cwmbran	15a
D	
Dagenham	19b
Dalbeattie	64d
Dale	21d
Daliburgh	103c
Dalkeith	74b
Dallas	94a
Dalleagles	72c
Dalmally	78b
Dalmellington	72c
Dalry (D & G)	64a
Dalry (S'clyde)	71b
Dalsetter	104b
Dalton	51b
Dalwhinnie	86a
Danbury	20a
Daresbury	46a
Darfield	48a
Darlington	60a
Dartford	19b
Dartmeet	4a
Dartmouth	4c
Darvel	72a
Darwen	52c
Dava	94c
Daventry	29b
Davidstow	5c
Daviot	93b
Dawley	35d
Dawlish	4b
Deal	14b
Debenham	41b
Deddington	29c
Deeping St.Nicholas	38a
Denbigh	45c
Denby Dale	47b
Denham	18b
Denholm	75d
Dennington	41b

Denny	80d	Drumnadrochit	92c
Denton	47a	Drumnaich	80a
Derby	36b	Drynoch	89d
Dereham	40a	Duddo	76c
Dersingham	39b	Dudley	35d
Dervaig	83d	Duffield	36b
Deskford	95b	Dufftown	95a
Devizes	16c	Duffus	94a
Devonport	3d	Duirnish	90c
Dewsbury	54c	Dulnain Bridge	94c
Diabaig	90a	Dulverton	6b
Dicker	12c	Dumbarton	79d
Didcot	17b	Dumfries	65a
Didmarton	16a	Dunbar	75b
Dingwall	92a	Dunbeath	100b
Dinnet	87b	Dunblane	80b
Dirleton	82d	Dunbridge	9b
Diss	32b	Dundee	82a
Distington	57a	Dundonald	72a
Ditton Priors	35c	Dundrennan	64d
Docking	39b	Dunfermline	81d
Docklow	27b	Dunholme	49b
Doddington	38d	Dunkeld	86d
Dolbenmaen	43d	Dunlop	72a
Dolgellau	33a	Dunnet	101b
Dollar	81d	Dunning	81b
Dolphinton	74a	Dunoon	78d
Dolwyddelan	44c	Duns	75b
Doncaster	48b	Dunstable	30c
Donington (Lincs)	38a	Dunster	7a
Dorchester (Dorset)	8c	Dunsyre	74a
Dorchester (Oxon)	17b	Dunvegan	89a
Dores	93c	Dunwich	41d
Dorking	11b	Durham	60a
Dornie	90d	Durness	98d
Dornoch	99a	Dursley	16a
Dorrington	34d	Durston	7b
Douglas (Strathclyde)	73d	Durweston	8b
Douglas (I.of M.)	51c	Duthil	93d
Dounby	101d	Dyce	96c
Doune	80d	Dykehead	87d
Dounreay	100d	Dymchurch	14c
Dover	14b	Dymock	27d
Dowally	86d	Dysart	82c
Downham Market	39c		
Downton	9b	**E**	
Draycott	36a		
Drayton	42b	Eaglesham	73a
Drem	82d	Eaglesham	72a
Droitwich	28a	Earby	53a
Dronfield	48a	Earls Colne	32c
Drumbeg	98a	Earlston	75d
Drummore	63d	Easdale	78a

Easebourne	11a	Eltham	19d
Easington	68d	Elton	38c
East Barkwith	50a	Elvanfoot	73d
East Bridgford	37b	Elvington	55a
Eastbourne	12d	Elworthy	7a
East Cowes	10c	Ely	31b
Eastchurch	20d	Embleton	76d
Eastdean	12d	Emsworth	10b
East Grinstead	12a	Enfield	19b
East Hoathley	12c	Epping	19b
East Horsley	11b	Epsom	19c
Easthampstead	18c	Epworth	49a
Easthampton	18c	Eriboll	98d
East Kilbride	72b	Errogie	92c
Eastleigh	10a	Erwood	26c
East Linton	82d	Esher	18d
East Lulworth	8d	Etal	76c
East Markham	49c	Ettington	28b
East Retford	48b	Ettrickbridge End	75c
Eastriggs	65d	Evanton	92a
Eastry	14b	Evelix	99a
East Wemyss	82c	Evercreech	8a
Eastwood	48c	Everingham	55d
Eaton Socon	30b	Evesham	28c
Ebbw Vale	24b	Ewenny	24c
Ebchester	68c	Ewhurst	11b
Ecclefechan	65b	Exbourne	3b
Eccleshall	35b	Exeter	4b
Echt	96c	Exford	6b
Eckington	48a	Exminster	4a
Edderton	99a	Exmouth	4b
Eddlestone	74a	Eye	41b
Edenbridge	12a	Eyemouth	76a
Edgcumbe	1d	Eynsford	19d
Edgware	19a	Eynsham	17b
Edinbane	89b		
Edinburgh	74a	**F**	
Edzell	88c		
Egham	18d	Fairford	16b
Eglingham	76d	Fairlie	71b
Egremont	57a	Fakenham	39b
Eilean Iarmain	90c	Falkirk	80d
Elgin	94a	Falkland	82a
Elgol	89d	Falmer	12c
Elie	82c	Falmouth	2c
Elland	53d	Falstone	66b
Ellesmere	34b	Fangfoss	55b
Ellesmere Port	45b	Fareham	10a
Ellon	96c	Faringdon	17a
Elphin	97d	Farnborough (London)	19d
Elrick	96c	Farnborough (Hants)	11a
Elstow	30a	Farndon	45d
Elstree	19a	Farnham	11a

a	b		
c	d		

Farnham Royal	18a	Folkingham	38a
Farnworth	46a	Fontmell Magna	8b
Faversham	13b	Ford	76c
Fawley	10c	Fordham	31b
Fazeley	36c	Fordingbridge	9b
Fearn	93b	Forest Row	12a
Fearnan	86c	Forfar	87d
Featherstone	54c	Formby	45b
Felbridge	12a	Fornham St.Martin	32a
Felixstowe	41c	Forres	94a
Felling	68c	Fort Augustus	92a
Felpham	11c	Fort George	93b
Felton	68a	Fort William	85a
Feltwell	39d	Fortinghall	86c
Fenstanton	31a	Fortrose	93b
Fenwick	72a	Fortuneswell	8c
Feolin	69b	Four Oaks	36c
Ferndown	9c	Fovant	9a
Fernhurst	11a	Fowey	2b
Ferrybridge	54c	Foxholes	56a
Ferryhill	60a	Foyers	92c
Ferryside	22d	Fraddon	2a
Fettercairn	88a	Framlingham	41b
Ffestiniog	44c	Frant	13c
Ffostrasol	22b	Fraserburgh	96b
Filby	42d	Freshwater	9d
Filey	56a	Fressingfield	41b
Filton	15b	Freswick	101b
Finborough	41b	Fridaythorpe	55b
Finchingfield	31d	Frinton	32d
Finchley	19a	Friockheim	88c
Findhorn	94a	Frodsham	46a
Findochty	95b	Frome	16c
Findon	11d	Frosterley	60a
Finedon	30a	Fulford	55a
Finnart	79d	Fulwood	52c
Finstown	101c	Fyfield	19b
Fionnphort	77a	Fyvie	96c
Fishbourne	10c		
Fishguard	21b	**G**	
Fishnish	84c		
Fiskavaig	89d	Gaerwen	43b
Fittleworth	11b	Gailey	35b
Flamborough	56a	Gainford	60a
Flax Bourton	15d	Gainsborough	49a
Fleet	18c	Gairloch	90a
Fleetwood	51b	Gairlochy	85a
Flimby	57a	Gairlogie	96c
Flimwell	13c	Galashiels	75c
Flint	45d	Galgate	51b
Flitsham	39b	Galson	103b
Flyford Flavell	28a	Galston	72a
Folkestone	14c	Gardenstown	96a

Garforth	54c
Gargrave	53a
Garlieston	64c
Garlogie	88b
Garmouth	94b
Garstang	51b
Garston	45b
Garth (Powys)	26a
Garth (Mid Glam)	24c
Gartmore	80c
Gartocharn	79d
Garvald	82d
Garve	92a
Garynahine	103b
Gatehouse of Fleet	64c
Gateshead	68c
Geddington	37d
Gedney Drove End	39a
George Nympton	6a
Gerrards Cross	18a
Giffnock	73a
Gifford	82d
Gilfach Goch	24c
Gillingham (Dorset)	8b
Gillingham (Kent)	20c
Gills	101b
Gilwern	26d
Girtford	30b
Girvan	63b
Gisburn	53a
Glamis	87d
Glasgow	73a
Glastonbury	8a
Glenbarr	70c
Glenbrittle	89d
Glencarse	81b
Glencoe	85c
Glendevon	81b
Glenelg	90c
Glenfinnan	84b
Glenluce	63d
Glenrothes	82c
Glossop	47b
Gloucester	28c
Glyn Neath	24a
Glyncorrwg	24a
Glyntaw	23b
Gnoshall	35b
Goathland	62c
Godalming	11a
Godmanchester	30b
Godshill (Hants)	9b
Godshill (I.of W.)	10c
Godstone	12a
Goginan	33c
Golders Green	19a
Golspie	99d
Goodwick	21b
Goole	55d
Gordonstoun	94a
Gorebridge	74b
Goring	17b
Gorleston	42c
Gosfield	32c
Gosforth	68c
Gosport	10c
Goudhurst	13d
Gourock	79d
Govan	73a
Gramisdale	103c
Grampound	2a
Grange (Cumbria)	51b
Grangemouth	81c
Grantham	37b
Granthouse	76a
Grantown-on-Spey	94c
Grasmere	57b
Grassington	53b
Gravesend	20a
Grayrigg	58c
Great Ayton	61d
Great Baddow	20a
Great Bradfield	31d
Great Chart	13b
Great Chesterford	31c
Great Driffield	56a
Great Dunmow	31d
Great Harwood	52c
Great Malvern	27b
Great Missenden	18a
Great Musgrave	59b
Great Offley	30d
Great Smeaton	60d
Greatstone-on-Sea	14c
Great Torrington	5b
Great Weldon	37d
Great Witley	27b
Great Yarmouth	42d
Green Hammerton	54a
Greenfield	45a
Greenhead	66d
Greenlaw	75d
Greenloaning	80b
Greenock	79d
Greenodd	57d
Greenwich	19b

Gretna	65d	Haroldswick	104b
Gretna Green	65d	Harpenden	30d
Greystoke	58a	Harrietsham	20c
Grimsby	50a	Harrogate	54a
Gringley on the Hill	49a	Harrow	18b
Grinton	60c	Hart	61b
Grizebeck	57d	Hartfield	12a
Groby	37c	Hartland	5b
Groombridge	12a	Hartlebury	28a
Gruinard	97a	Hartlepool	60b
Gruinart	69a	Hartley Wintney	18c
Guildford	11b	Harwell	17b
Guisborough	61b	Harwich	32d
Guiseley	53d	Hascombe	11a
Gullane	82c	Haslemere	11a
Gunnislake	3b	Haslingden	52c
Guyhirn	38d	Hastings	13d
Gwbert-on-Sea	22a	Hatfield (Herts)	19a
		Hatfield (S.Yorks)	48b
H		Hatherleigh	6c
		Hathersage	47b
Haddenham	31a	Havant	10b
Haddington	75a	Haverfordwest	21d
Hadleigh (Suffolk)	32c	Haverhill	31b
Hadleigh (Essex)	20a	Hawes	59d
Hailsham	12d	Hawick	75c
Hale	46b	Hawkhurst	13d
Halesowen	28a	Hawkshead	57d
Halesworth	40d	Haworth	53d
Halford	28b	Haxey	49a
Halifax	53d	Hay-on-Wye	26d
Halkirk	100d	Haydon Bridge	67d
Halland	12c	Hayle	1d
Halloughton	48d	Haytor Vale	4a
Hallsands	4c	Haywards Heath	12a
Halstead	32c	Heacham	39b
Halton Gill	52b	Headcorn	13b
Haltwhistle	66d	Heanor	36b
Halwell	4c	Heathfield	13c
Ham Street	13d	Hebden Bridge	53d
Hamble	10a	Heckfield	18c
Hambledon	10a	Heckington	38a
Hamilton	73a	Heckmondwike	53d
Hampstead	19a	Heddon on the Wall	68c
Hampton	18d	Hedon	56c
Handsworth (Yorks)	48a	Heiton	75d
Hanley	46d	Helensburgh	79d
Harbottle	67b	Helmsdale	99b
Hardwicke	27d	Helmsley	61d
Harlech	44c	Helsby	46a
Harleston	42a	Helston	1d
Harlow	19b	Hemel Hempstead	18b
Harmerhill	34b	Hemsby	42d

Hendon	19a
Henfield	11d
Henley in Arden	28b
Henley-on-Thames	18a
Henlow	30d
Henstridge	8b
Hereford	27c
Hermitage	17d
Herne	14a
Herne Bay	14a
Hertford	19b
Hessle	56c
Heswall	45b
Hethersett	42a
Hetton le Hole	68d
Hexham	67d
Heysham	51b
Heywood	46b
Hibaldstow	49b
High Bentham	52a
Highclere	17c
High Hampton	5d
High Hawsker	62c
High Hesket	58a
High Wycombe	18a
Highworth	16b
Hilborough	39d
Hilderthorpe	56a
Hillswick	104a
Hinckley	36d
Hinderwell	62a
Hindhead	11a
Hindley	46a
Hintlesham	32b
Hirwaun	24a
Histon	31a
Hitchin	30d
Hobkirk	75d
Hockering	42b
Hoddesdon	19a
Hodnet	35a
Holbeach	38b
Holkham	39b
Holme (Cumbria)	58c
Holme (Humberside)	55d
Holmes Chapel	46d
Holmfirth	47b
Holsworthy	3a
Holt	40a
Holyhead	43b
Holytown	73b
Holywell	45c
Homersfield	42a

Honington	32a
Honiton	7d
Hook (Hants)	18c
Hope Bowdler	34d
Hope under Dinmore	27a
Horbury	54c
Horley	12a
Horncastle	50c
Horndean	10b
Hornden	20a
Horns Cross	5b
Hornsea	56a
Horsforth	54c
Horsham	11b
Horton in Ribblesdale	52b
Horwich	46a
Houghton-le-Spring	68d
Hounslow	18d
Hove	12c
Hovingham	55a
Howden	55d
Hownam	75d
Hoxne	41b
Hoylake	45b
Hucknall	48c
Huddersfield	53d
Huggate	55b
Hull	56c
Humberstone	50a
Huna	101b
Hunford	72a
Hungerford	17c
Hunmanby	56a
Hunstanton	39b
Huntingdon	30b
Huntley	95b
Hurstbourne Tarrant	17c
Hurstmonceux	13c
Hurstpierpoint	12c
Hurworth	61a
Husbands Bosworth	37c
Hutton Rudby	61d
Hyde	47a
Hythe (Kent)	14c
Hythe (Hants)	10a

I

Ibsley	9b
Ibstock	36b
Ilchester	8a
Ilfracombe	6a
Ilkestone	36b

Ilkley	53d
Ilminster	7b
Immingham	56c
Inchbare	88c
Inchnadamph	97d
Inchture	82a
Indian Queens	2a
Inellan	79d
Ingatestone	20a
Ingbirchworth	47b
Ingleton	52a
Ingoldmells	50d
Innerleithen	74d
Insch	95d
Insh	86a
Inveralligin	90a
Inverallochy	96b
Inveraray	78b
Inverbeg	79d
Inverbervie	88c
Inverewe	97a
Inverey	87a
Inverfarigaig	92c
Invergarry	85b
Invergordon	93b
Inverinate	91c
Inverkeilor	88c
Inverkeithing	81d
Inverkip	71b
Inverkirkaig	97b
Invermoriston	92c
Inverness	93a
Inversanda	84d
Invershiel	90d
Invershin	99a
Inversnaid	79b
Inverurie	96c
Ipswich	32b
Irlam	46a
Ironbridge	35c
Irthlingborough	30a
Irvine	71b
Isbister	104a
Isle of Whithorn	64c
Isleham	31b
Itchen	10a
Itchen Stoke	10a
Ivybridge	3d
Ivychurch	14d

J

Jamestown	79d

Jarrow	68d
Jedburgh	75d
John o' Groats	101b
Johnston	21d
Johnstone	72a

K

Kames	78d
Kegworth	37a
Keighley	53d
Keills	77d
Keiss	101b
Keith	95b
Keld	59d
Kelham	49c
Kellybray	2a
Kelmarsh	29b
Kelsall	46c
Kelso	75d
Kelty	81d
Kelvedon	32c
Kemnay	96c
Kempston	30a
Kendal	58c
Kenilworth	28b
Kenmore	86c
Kenn	15c
Kennacraig	70a
Kenninghall	42a
Kessingland	42c
Kessock	92b
Keston	19d
Keswick	57b
Kettering	30a
Kettlebridge	82a
Kettlewell	53b
Keynsham	15d
Kibworth Harcourt	37d
Kidderminster	28a
Kidlington	29c
Kidsgrove	47b
Kidwelly	22d
Kilbarchan	72a
Kilberry	70a
Kilbirnie	71b
Kilburn	61d
Kilchattan	71b
Kilchenzie	70c
Kilchoan	83d
Kilchrenan	78b
Kilconquhar	82a
Kilcreggan	79d

Kildonan	99d	Kippford	65c
Kilfinan	78c	Kirby Hill	54a
Kilkhampton	5d	Kirby Malzeard	53b
Killean	70a	Kirkaldy	82c
Killimster	101b	Kirkbampton	65d
Killin	80a	Kirkbean	65c
Killingworth	68c	Kirkbride	65d
Kilmalcom	71b	Kirkby	45b
Kilmaluag	89b	Kirkby Lonsdale	58c
Kilmarnock	72a	Kirkbymoorside	62c
Kilmartin	78c	Kirkby Stephen	59b
Kilmaurs	72a	Kirkcolm	63a
Kilmelford	78a	Kirkconnel	72d
Kilmichael	78c	Kirk Deighton	54a
Kilmorach	92a	Kirkfieldbank	73b
Kilmory	78c	Kirkham	51d
Kilmun	79d	Kirkliston	74a
Kilninver	78a	Kirkmichael	87c
Kilnsea	56d	Kirknewton	76c
Kilrenny	82b	Kirkoswald	71d
Kilsby	29b	Kirkpatrick Fleming	65d
Kilwinning	71b	Kirkudbright	64d
Kimberley	42a	Kirkwall	101d
Kinbrace	100c	Kirriemuir	87d
Kincardine	81d	Kirton (Humberside)	49b
Kincardine O'Neil	88a	Kirton (Lincs)	38b
Kincraig	86b	Knaresborough	54a
Kinghorn	82c	Knarsdale	66d
Kingsbarns	82b	Knighton	26b
Kingsbridge	4c	Knockandhu	94c
Kingsclere	17d	Knottingley	54c
Kingsdown	19d	Knutsford	46b
Kingsgate	14b	Kyle of Lochalsh	90c
King's Heath	36c	Kyleakin	90c
King's Langley	18b	Kylerhea	90c
King's Lynn	39a	Kylestrome	98c
Kings Norton	28a		
Kings Somborne	9b	**L**	
Kingsteignton	4a		
Kingston Bagpuize	17a	Laceby	50a
Kingston upon Thames	18d	Lacock	16c
Kingswear	4c	Ladbroke	29a
Kingussie	86a	Ladybank	82a
Kinlochbervie	98d	Lagg	77d
Kinlochewe	90b	Laggan Bridge	86a
Kinloch Hourn	84b	Laide	97a
Kinlochleven	85c	Lairg	99a
Kinlochmoidart	84a	Lakenheath	39d
Kinloch Rannoch	86c	Lamberhurst	13c
Kinloss	94a	Lambourn	17a
Kinross	81b	Lamlash	70d
Kintore	96c	Lampeter	25b
Kippax	54c	Lamphey	21d

Lanark	73b	Leslie	82a
Lancaster	51b	Lesmahagow	73b
Lanchester	68c	Letchworth	30d
Landford	9b	Letheringsett	40a
Lands End	1c	Leuchars	82a
Lane End	18a	Leven	82c
Langholm	66a	Leven	56c
Langport	7b	Leverburgh	103c
Langtoft	56a	Lewes	12c
Lanivet	2a	Lewisham	19b
Lapford	6c	Leyburn	60c
Larbert	81c	Leyland	52c
Largo	82a	Leysdown	20d
Largo Ward	82a	Lhanbryde	94b
Largs	71b	Libberton	73b
Larkhall	73b	Lichfield	36a
Larling	40c	Lifton	3b
Lastingham	62c	Lilliesleaf	75c
Latheron	101a	Limpsfield	12a
Lauder	75a	Lincoln	49d
Laugharne	22c	Lindores	82a
Laughton	12c	Lingdale	62a
Launceston	3a	Linlithgow	73b
Laurencekirk	88a	Linslade	30c
Laurieston	64c	Lintmill	95b
Lavenham	32a	Linton	31b
Lawers	86c	Linwood	72a
Lawton	46d	Liphook	10b
Laxey	51c	Liskeard	3c
Lazonby	58a	Liss	10b
Leadburn	74a	Littleborough	53c
Leadenham	49d	Littlebourne	14a
Leadgate	68c	Littlehampton	11d
Leadhills	73d	Little Ouseburn	54a
Leasingham	49d	Littleport	39c
Leatherhead	18d	Littlestone-on-Sea	14c
Lechlade	16b	Little Stukeley	30b
Leconfield	56c	Little Thurlow	31b
Ledbury	27d	Liverpool	45b
Lee on the Solent	10c	Liversedge	53d
Leeds	54c	Lizard	1d
Leedstown	1d	Llanaber	33a
Leek	47c	Llanaelhaearn	43d
Leeming	61c	Llanbedr	33a
Legbourne	50a	Llanbedrog	43d
Leicester	37c	Llanberis	44a
Leigh (Grtr Manchester)	46a	Llanbrynmair	33d
Leigh on Sea	20a	Llanddewi	23c
Leighton Buzzard	30c	Llandeilo	23b
Leiston	41d	Llandinam	34c
Lendalfoot	63b	Llandissilio	22a
Leominster	27a	Llandovery	23b
Lerwick	104b	Llandrillo	44b

Llandrindod Wells	26a	Lochgilphead	78c
Llandudno	44a	Lochgoilhead	79d
Llandyssul	22b	Lochinver	97b
Llanelli	22d	Lochmaben	65b
Llanerchymedd	43b	Lochmaddy	103c
Llanfaethlu	43b	Lochranza	70a
Llanfair Caereinion	34c	Lochwinnoch	71b
Llanfairfechan	44a	Lockerbie	65b
Llanfair Talhaiarn	44b	Loddon	42c
Llanfihangel	26d	Loftus	62a
Llanfrynach	26c	Loggerheads	35b
Llanfyllin	34a	Logierait	86d
Llangadog	23b	London	19a
Llangamarch Wells	26a	London Colney	18b
Llangefni	43b	Long Bennington	37b
Llangelynin	33c	Longbenton	68c
Llangennith	22d	Long Compton	28d
Llangoed	44a	Long Crendon	17b
Llangollen	34a	Long Eaton	37a
Llangurig	33d	Longforgan	82a
Llangwnnadl	43c	Longformacus	75b
Llangybi	25b	Longframlington	68a
Llangynog	34a	Longhorsley	68a
Llanidloes	33d	Longhoughton	68a
Llanmadoc	22d	Long Newton	60b
Llanon	23a	Longniddry	82c
Llanrwst	44b	Long Preston	53a
Llansantffraid	25a	Longridge	52c
Llansawel	25d	Long Sutton (Lincs)	39a
Llansoy	15a	Long Sutton (Somerset)	8a
Llanthony	26d	Longtown	66c
Llantrisant	24c	Looe, E. & W.	3c
Llantwit Major	24c	Lossiemouth	94b
Llanuwchllyn	33b	Lostwithiel	2b
Llanwrtyd Wells	26a	Loughborough	37a
Llanybyther	25c	Louth	50a
Llanymynech	34a	Lowestoft	42c
Llanyre	26a	Lowick	76c
Llechryd	22a	Ludag	103c
Lledrod	25b	Ludgershall	17c
Llwyngwril	33a	Ludlow	27a
Llyswen	26c	Lumphanan	88a
Loanhead	74a	Lumsden	95d
Loans	71d	Luss	79d
Lochailort	84a	Luton	30d
Lochaline	84c	Lutterworth	29b
Locharbriggs	65a	Lybster	101c
Lochboisdale	103c	Lydd	14c
Lochbuie	77b	Lydford	3b
Lochcarron	90b	Lydney	15b
Lochearnhead	80a	Lyme Regis	7d
Lochgair	78c	Lyminge	14a
Lochgelly	81d	Lymington	9d

Lymm	46a	Markfield	37a
Lympne	14c	Markinch	82c
Lyndhurst	9b	Marksbury	15d
Lyneham	16a	Marlborough	16d
Lyness	101c	Marlow	18d
Lynmouth	6a	Marple	47a
Lynton	6a	Marsden (W.Yorks)	47b
Lytchett Minster	9c	Marshfield	16a
Lytham St.Annes	51d	Martock	8b
		Marton (Lincs)	49a
M		Maryculter	88b
		Marykirk	88c
Mablethorpe	50b	Maryport	57a
Macclesfield	46d	Masham	61c
Macduff	95b	Matlock	47d
Machen	24d	Mauchline	72c
Machrihanish	69d	Maxton	75d
Machynlleth	33c	Maybole	71d
Mackworth	36b	Mayfield	13c
Macmerry	74d	Measham	36b
Maesteg	23d	Meigle	87d
Maghull	45b	Meikleour	87c
Magor	15a	Melbourn	31a
Maiden Bradley	8b	Melbourne	36b
Maidenhead	18a	Melksham	16c
Maiden Newton	8c	Mellon Charles	97a
Maidens	71d	Melness	100b
Maidstone	13b	Melrose	75d
Maldon	20a	Melsonby	60c
Malham	53d	Meltham	47b
Mallaig	84a	Melton Mowbray	37b
Malmesbury	16a	Melvaig	97a
Malpas	34b	Melvich	100d
Maltby	48a	Menai Bridge	44a
Malton	55b	Meopham	20c
Malvern Wells	27d	Mere	8b
Manchester	47a	Merrivale	2b
Mangotsfield	15b	Merthyr Tydfil	24a
Manningtree	32d	Messingham	49b
Manorbier	21d	Methil	82c
Mansfield	48c	Methlick	96c
Marazion	1c	Methven	81b
March	38d	Methwold	39d
Maresfield	12a	Mettingham	42c
Margam	23d	Mevagissey	2a
Margate	14b	Mexborough	48a
Mark	15c	Mid Calder	74a
Market Deeping	38a	Middleham	60c
Market Drayton	35a	Middlemarsh	8a
Market Harborough	37d	Middlesbrough	61b
Market Rasen	49b	Middleton (Norfolk)	39b
Market Warsop	48c	Middleton in Teesdale	59b
Market Weighton	55d	Middlewich	46c

Midgeholme	66d
Midhurst	11c
Mid-Lavant	11c
Midsomer Norton	15d
Mid Yell	104b
Mildenhall	31b
Milford (Surrey)	11a
Milford Haven	21d
Millerston	72b
Millmeece	35b
Millom	57d
Millport	71b
Milnathort	81b
Milnthorpe	51b
Milovaig	89a
Milton	9d
Milton Abbot	3b
Milton Keynes	30c
Milverton	7a
Minehead	6b
Minster (Kent, I.of Sheppey)	20d
Minster (Kent)	14a
Minsterley	34d
Mintlaw	96b
Mirfield	53d
Misterton (Notts)	49a
Misterton (Somerset)	8a
Mitford	68a
Mobberley	46b
Modbury	3d
Moelfre	44a
Moffat	74c
Mold	45d
Moniaive	64b
Monifieth	82b
Monkleigh	5b
Monks Eleigh	41a
Monkton	72c
Monmouth	27c
Montgomery	34c
Montrose	88c
Monyash	47d
Monymusk	95d
Morar	84a
Morecambe	51b
Moresby	57a
Moreton in Marsh	28d
Moretonhampstead	4a
Morley	54c
Morpeth	68a
Morriston	23b
Mortehoe	5b
Mortimers Cross	27a
Mossat	94d
Motherwell	73b
Mountain Ash	24a
Mountsorrel	37a
Mousehole	1c
Mouswald	65d
Mowtie	88b
Muchalls	88b
Much Birch	27c
Much Hadham	31c
Much Wenlock	35c
Muddleswood	11d
Muir of Fowlis	95d
Muir of Ord	92a
Muirdrum	82b
Muirhead	82a
Muirkirk	73c
Muker	59d
Mullion	1d
Mumbles	23d
Mumby	50d
Mundesley	40b
Munlochy	93a
Murlaggan	84b
Musselburgh	74b
Muthill	81a
Mybster	101b

N

Nafferton	56a
Nailsea	15d
Nailsworth	16a
Nairn	93b
Nant-y-Moel	24c
Nantgarw	24c
Nantwich	46c
Narberth	22c
Narborough	37c
Neath	23d
Needham Market	32b
Neilston	72a
Nelson (Lancs)	52d
Nelson (Mid Glam)	24a
Nenthead	67d
Nenthorn	75d
Nesscliff	34b
Neston	45b
Nether Stowey	7b
Netherwitten	68a
Nethy Bridge	94c
New Abbey	65c
New Aberdour	96a

Newark-on-Trent	49c
Newbiggin-by-the-Sea	68a
Newbigging	73b
Newbridge	24b
Newbridge-on-Wye	26a
Newburgh	82a
Newburgh	96d
Newburn	68c
Newbury	17d
Newcastle Emlyn	22a
Newcastle-under-Lyme	35b
Newcastle-upon-Tyne	68c
Newcastleton	66a
New Cumnock	72c
New Deer	96a
Newent	27d
New Galloway	64a
Newhaven	12c
New Holland	56c
Newingreen	14c
Newlyn	1c
Newmachar	96c
Newmarket	31b
New Mills	47a
Newmilns	72a
Newnham	27d
New Pitsligo	96a
Newport (Salop)	35b
Newport (Dyfed)	21b
Newport (Gwent)	15a
Newport (I.o.W.)	10c
Newport Pagnell	30c
Newport-on-Tay	82a
New Quay	25a
Newquay	2a
New Romney	14c
New Scone	81b
New Seaham	68d
Newton Abbot	4a
Newton Arlosh	65d
Newton Aycliffe	60a
Newton Ferrers	3d
Newtongrange	75a
Newton-le-Willows	46a
Newton on the Moor	68a
Newtonmore	86a
Newton Poppleford	7c
Newton Stewart	64c
Newtown	34c
Newtown St. Boswells	75d
Newtyle	87d
Neyland	21d
Nigg	93b
Ninfield	13c
Nordelph	39c
Norham	76c
Norman Cross	38c
Normanton	54c
Northallerton	60d
Northampton	29b
North Bersted	11c
North Berwick	82d
North Cave	55d
North Elmhall	40a
North Ferriby	55d
North Frodingham	56a
Northiam	13d
Northleach	28d
North Petherton	7b
Northolt	18b
North Queensferry	81d
North Somercotes	50a
North Sunderland	76d
North Tawton	6c
North Thoresby	50a
North Tidworth	16d
North Tolsta	103b
North Walsham	40b
Northwich	46c
Norwich	40b
Nottingham	37a
Nuneaton	36d
Nunthorpe	61b
Nutley	12a

O

Oadby	37c
Oakham	37d
Oakhill	15d
Oakworth	53d
Oban	78a
Occumster	101a
Ochiltree	72c
Ockley	11b
Ogmore	24c
Okehampton	3b
Old Dailly	63b
Oldham	47a
Old Leake	50c
Oldmeldrum	96c
Ollaberry	104a
Ollerton	48d
Olney	30a
Onchan	51c
Ordie	87b

Orford	41c
Ormesby St. Margaret	42d
Ormiston	82c
Ormskirk	45b
Orpington	19d
Orton	59a
Ossett	54c
Ossington	48d
Oswaldkirk	54b
Oswaldtwistle	52c
Oswestry	34b
Otford	19d
Otley	53d
Otterbourne	10a
Otterburn	67b
Otter Ferry	78c
Otterswick	104b
Ottery St. Mary	7c
Oundle	38c
Outwell	39c
Overbister	101d
Overstrand	40a
Overton (Clwyd)	34b
Overton (Hants)	17d
Over Whiteacre	36c
Oxford	17b
Oykel Bridge	97d

P

Paddock Wood	13a
Padstow	2a
Paignton	4c
Painswick	16a
Paisley	72a
Pangbourne	17b
Parkeston	32d
Parracombe	6a
Paston	40b
Pateley Bridge	53b
Pathhead	74b
Patna	72c
Patrington	56a
Peak Forest	47b
Peasemarsh	13d
Peasenhall	41d
Peebles	74a
Peel	51c
Pembroke	21d
Pembroke Dock	21d
Pembury	13a
Penally	22c
Penarth	24d

Pencaitland	75a
Penderyn	24a
Pendine	22c
Penegoes	33d
Penicuik	74a
Penistone	47b
Penketh	46a
Penkridge	35b
Penmaenmawr	44a
Pennal	33c
Penrith	58a
Penryn	2c
Pensford	15d
Penshurst	12a
Pentraeth	44a
Pentrebont	25b
Pentre-Foelas	44d
Penzance	1c
Perranporth	1b
Pershore	28a
Perth	81b
Peterborough	38c
Peterculter	88b
Peterhead	96b
Peterlee	60b
Petersfield	10b
Petworth	11a
Pevensey	12d
Pewsey	16d
Philleigh	2c
Pickering	55b
Piddletrenthide	8c
Piercebridge	61a
Pierowall	101d
Pinchbeck	38a
Piperspool	3a
Pirnmill	70a
Pitlochry	86d
Pitscottie	82a
Pitsea	20a
Pittentrail	99b
Pittenweem	82d
Playden	13d
Plean	80d
Plockton	90c
Pluckley	13b
Plymouth	3d
Plympton	3d
Pocklington	55b
Polbathic	3c
Polegate	12d
Polmont	81d
Polperro	2b

Polzeath	2a	Prestatyn	45a
Ponders End	19b	Presteigne	26b
Pontardawe	23b	Preston (Lancs)	52c
Pontardulais	23b	Preston (Dorset)	8c
Pontefract	54c	Preston Brockhurst	35a
Ponteland	68c	Preston Candover	10a
Pontrhydfendigaid	25b	Prestonpans	82c
Pontyates	23a	Prestwick	71d
Pontypool	15a	Princes Risborough	18a
Pontypridd	24c	Princetown	3b
Poole	9c	Probus	2a
Poolewe	97a	Prudhoe	68c
Porlock	6b	Puckeridge	31c
Port Appin	84d	Puddletown	8d
Port Askaig	69b	Pudsey	53c
Port Bannantyne	71b	Pulborough	11b
Port Charlotte	69a	Pulham	42a
Port Ellen	69a	Purfleet	19b
Port Erin	51c	Purton	16b
Port Glasgow	79d	Pwllheli	43d
Portgower	99d	Pycombe	12c
Porth	24c		
Porth-y-Rhydd	22d	**Q**	
Porthcawl	23d		
Porthleven	1d	Queenborough	20d
Porthmadog	33a	Queensferry	45d
Porthowen	1b	Quorn	37a
Port Isaac	2a		
Portishead	15a	**R**	
Portknockie	95b		
Portlethen	88b	Radcliffe (Grtr Manchester)	46b
Portloe	2c	Radcliffe on Trent	37a
Port Logan	63c	Radlett	19a
Portmahomack	99c	Radstock	15d
Portnacroish	84d	Raglan	15a
Portnaguiran	103b	Rainford	46a
Portnahaven	69d	Rainham	19b
Port of Menteith	80a	Rampside	51b
Port of Ness	103b	Ramsbottom	52a
Portpatrick	63c	Ramsey (Cambs)	38d
Portree	89b	Ramsey (I.o.M.)	51c
Portskerra	100c	Ramsgate	14b
Portsmouth	10d	Ranby	48b
Portsonachan	78b	Rapness	101d
Portsoy	95b	Rathen	96b
Port Talbot	23d	Ratlinghope	34d
Port William	63d	Rattray	87d
Potterne	16c	Raund	30a
Potter's Bar	19a	Ravenglass	57d
Potton	30b	Ravenscar	62d
Poulton-le-Fylde	51d	Rawcliffe	55c
Prees	35a	Rawmarsh	48a
Prescot	46a	Rawtenstall	52d

Rayleigh	20a	Romanno Bridge	74a
Reading	17d	Romford	19b
Reculver	14a	Romiley	47a
Redcar	61b	Romsey	9b
Redcastle	92a	Ropley	10a
Redditch	28a	Rosehearty	96a
Redhill	12a	Rosemarkie	92b
Redruth	1d	Roskhill	89a
Reedham	42c	Roslin	74a
Reepham	42b	Ross-on-Wye	27d
Reeth	60c	Rosyth	81d
Reigate	11b	Rothbury	67b
Reiss	101b	Rotherham	48a
Rempstone	37a	Rothesay	71b
Renfrew	72a	Rothes-on-Spey	94a
Repton	36b	Rothwell (W.Yorks)	54c
Resolven	23b	Rothwell (Northants)	37d
Revesby	50c	Rottingdean	12c
Reydon	41d	Roughton	40a
Rhayader	26a	Roxton	30b
Rhiconich	98c	Royal Leamington Spa	29a
Rhondda	24a	Royal Tunbridge Wells	12b
Rhosli	22d	Roybridge	85b
Rhosneigr	43a	Royston	31c
Rhos-on-Sea	44b	Royton	47a
Rhuddan	45a	Ruabon	45d
Rhyd-Owen	25a	Rudston	56a
Rhyl	44b	Rugby	29b
Rhymney	24a	Rugeley	36a
Rhyne	95d	Runcorn	46a
Richborough	14b	Rushden	30a
Richmond	60c	Ruskington	49d
Richmond upon Thames	18d	Rutherglen	72a
Rickmansworth	18b	Ruthin	45c
Riding Mill	67d	Ruthven	87d
Ridsdale	67b	Ryde	10c
Rievaulx	61d	Rye	13d
Ringford	64c	Ryhope	68d
Ringmer	12c	Rylstone	52b
Ringwood	9d	Ryton	68c
Ripley (Derbys)	48c		
Ripley (Surrey)	11b	**S**	
Ripon	54a		
Roade	29b	Sadberge	60b
Roberton	74d	Saffron Walden	31d
Robertsbridge	13c	St.Abbs	76a
Robin Hood's Bay	62d	St.Agnes	1b
Rochdale	52d	St.Albans	18b
Rochester	13a	St.Andrews	82b
Rochford	20a	St.Asaph	45c
Rock	2a	St.Austell	2a
Rodel	103b	St.Bees	57a
Rogate	11a	St.Blazey	2b

St.Buryan	1c	Saundersfoot	22c
St.Catherines	78b	Saxilby	49d
St.Clears	22c	Saxmundham	41d
St.Columb Major	2a	Scalby	62d
St.Columb Minor	2a	Scalloway	104c
St.Combs	96b	Scamblesby	50a
St.Cyrus	88c	Scampton	49b
St.Davids	21a	Scarborough	62d
St.Devereux	27c	Scarfskerry	101b
St.Fillans	80a	Scarinish	83a
St.Germans	3c	Scartho	50a
St.Helens (Merseyside)	46a	Scleddau	21b
St.Helens (I.of W.)	10c	Sconser	89d
St.Ives (Cornwall)	1d	Scotch Corner	61c
St.Ives (Huntingdon)	31a	Scotter	49b
St.John's Chapel	59b	Scourie	98c
St.Just	1c	Scousburgh	104c
St.Keverne	2c	Scrabster	101b
St.Leonards	13d	Scriven	54a
St.Margarets at Cliffe	14b	Scrooby	48b
St.Margaret's Hope	101c	Scunthorpe	49b
St.Marys (Orkney)	101c	Seaford	12c
St.Mawes	2c	Seaham	68d
St.Mellons	24d	Seahouses	76d
St.Monans	82b	Seal	19d
St.Neots	30b	Seamer	62d
St.Ninians	81c	Seamill	71b
St.Petrox	21d	Seascale	57c
Salcombe	4c	Seaton	7d
Sale	46b	Sedbergh	58d
Salen (Highland)	84c	Sedgefield	61b
Salen (Mull)	84c	Sedgley	35d
Salford	46b	Sedlescombe	13d
Saline	81d	Seend	16c
Salisbury	9b	Selborne	10b
Saltash	3d	Selby	54d
Saltburn	62a	Selkirk	75c
Saltcoats	71b	Sellindge	14c
Saltfleet	50a	Selly Oak	36c
Sanaigmore	69a	Selsey	11c
Sandbach	46d	Selstad	14a
Sandbank	79c	Semington	16c
Sandersted	19d	Sennen	1c
Sandgate	14c	Settle	53a
Sandhead	63c	Sevenoaks	13a
Sandown	10c	Severn Stoke	28c
Sandwich	14b	Shaftesbury	8b
Sandwick	104c	Shalbourne	17c
Sandy	30b	Shalford	11b
Sannox	70b	Shanklin	10c
Sanquhar	73d	Shap	59a
Sarre	14a	Sharpness	15b
Satley	60a	Sharwell	10c

Shawbury	35a	Slapton	4c
Sheerness	20b	Sleaford	49d
Sheffield	48a	Sledmere	55b
Shefford	30d	Sleights	62c
Shepton Mallet	8a	Slough	18a
Sherborne	8a	Slyne	51b
Sherburn in Elmet	54c	Smailholm	75d
Shere	11b	Smithfield	66c
Sheringham	40a	Smithwick	36c
Sherston	16a	Smoo	98d
Shieldaig	90a	Snaith	55c
Shifnal	35d	Snodland	13a
Shildon	60a	Soham	31b
Shillingford	17b	Solihull	28b
Shilton	36d	Solva	21a
Shipley	53d	Somerton	8a
Shipston on Stour	28d	Sompting	11d
Shipton-under-Wychwood	28d	Sonning	18c
Shoeburyness	20b	Sorn	72c
Shoreham by Sea	11d	Soulby	58b
Shotley	41a	Sourton	3b
Shotley Bridge	68c	Southall	18b
Shotton	45d	Southam	29a
Shotts	73b	Southampton	9b
Shrewsbury	34b	South Brent	4c
Shrivenham	17a	Southend-on-Sea	20a
Sidcot	15c	Southery	39c
Sidcup	19d	South Ferriby	55d
Siddington	46d	South Harting	10b
Sidford	7d	South Hayling	10d
Sidlesham	10d	South Kelsey	49b
Sidmouth	7c	South Kilvington	61d
Silkstone	47b	South Mimms	19a
Silloth	65d	Southminster	20b
Silsden	53b	South Molton	6a
Silverdale	51b	South Ockendon	19b
Silverstone	29d	South Otterington	61d
Simonburn	67d	South Petherton	7b
Simonsbath	6b	Southport	51d
Singleton	11c	South Queensferry	81d
Sissinghurst	13d	Southsea	10c
Sittingbourne	13b	South Shields	68d
Sixpenny Handley	9a	Southwell	48d
Skaill	101c	Southwold	41d
Skegness	50d	Sowerby Bridge	53d
Skelmersdale	46a	Spalding	38b
Skelmorlie	71b	Sparkford	8a
Skelton	61b	Spean Bridge	85a
Skewen	23b	Spennymoor	60a
Skipsea	56a	Spetchley	28a
Skipton	52d	Spey Bay	94b
Slaidburn	52a	Spilsby	50c
Slammanan	81c	Spinningdale	99a

Spittal	76a	Stoke-on-Trent	35b
Spittal of Glenshee	87c	Stokenchurch	18a
Spofforth	54a	Stokesay	27a
Springholm	64b	Stokesley	61d
Sproatley	56c	Stone (Staffs)	35b
Sprouston	75d	Stone (Glos)	15b
Stadhampton	17b	Stonehaven	88b
Staffin	89b	Stonehouse	16a
Stafford	35b	Stoneykirk	63c
Stagsden	30a	Stonor	18a
Staindrop	60a	Stony Stratford	29d
Staines	18d	Stornoway	103b
Staithes	62a	Storrington	11d
Stalbridge	8b	Stourbridge	28a
Stalybridge	47a	Stourport	27b
Stamford	38c	Stow (Borders)	75c
Stamford Bridge	54b	Stow on the Wold	28d
Standish	46a	Stowmarket	32a
Stanford le Hope	20c	Strachan	88a
Stanhope	59b	Stradsett	39d
Stanley (Durham)	68c	Stranraer	63c
Stanley (Tayside)	81b	Stratford St.Mary	32d
Stanlow	45b	Stratford-upon-Avon	28b
Stanmore	18b	Strathaven	72b
Stannington	68a	Strathcanaird	97d
Stanstead Abbots	19b	Strathmiglo	81b
Stansted	31d	Strathpeffer	92a
Stapleford	37a	Strathy	100d
Staplehurst	13b	Strathyre	80a
Starcross	4b	Stratton	5d
Staveley (Cumbria)	58c	Streatley	17b
Staveley (Derbys)	48c	Street	8a
Staxton	56a	Strensall	55a
Stein	89a	Stretford	46b
Stenhousemuir	80d	Strichen	96a
Stepps	73a	Stromeferry	90d
Stevenage	30d	Stromness	101d
Stevenston	71b	Stronachlachar	79b
Stewarton	72a	Stronmilchan	79b
Steyning	11d	Strontian	84c
Stibb Cross	5d	Stroud	16a
Stickney	50c	Struan	86c
Stiffkey	40a	Struy	92c
Stillington	54b	Studland	9c
Stilton	38c	Studley	28a
Stirling	80d	Sturminster Newton	8b
Stithians	1d	Sturry	14a
Stock	20a	Sturton	49b
Stockbridge	9b	Sudbury	32c
Stockport	46b	Sumburgh	104c
Stocksbridge	47b	Summer Bridge	53b
Stockton-on-Tees	60b	Sunderland	68d
Stoke Mandeville	18a	Surbiton	18d

Sutton	19c
Sutton Benger	16a
Sutton Bridge	39a
Sutton Coldfield	36c
Sutton in Ashfield	48c
Sutton on Sea	50b
Swadlincote	36b
Swainsthorpe	42a
Swanage	9c
Swansea	23d
Swindon	16b
Swineshead	38a
Swinton (Grtr Manchester)	46b
Swinton (Borders)	76a
Symington	73d
Symonds Yat	27d
Syston	37a

T

Tadcaster	54c
Tadley	17d
Tain	99c
Talerddig	33d
Talley	23b
Talybont	33c
Tamworth	36c
Tannadice	87d
Tarbert (W.Isles)	103b
Tarbert (Strathclyde)	70a
Tarbolton	72c
Tarporley	46c
Tarrant Hinton	9a
Tarskavaig	84a
Tarves	96c
Tarvin	46c
Tattershall	50c
Taunton	7b
Tavistock	3b
Taynuilt	78b
Tayport	82a
Tayvallich	78c
Teangue	90c
Tedburn St.Mary	4a
Teignmouth	4a
Telford	35a
Templand	65b
Templecombe	8a
Temple Ewell	14b
Tenbury Wells	27b
Tenby	22c
Tenterden	13d
Terrington	54b

Terrington St.Clement	39a
Tetbury	16a
Tewkesbury	28c
Thame	17b
Thamesmead	19b
Thatcham	17d
Thetford	32a
The Witterings	10d
Thirsk	54a
Thornaby-on-Tees	60b
Thornbury	15b
Thorne	55c
Thornhill	64b
Thornton	82c
Thornton Curtis	56c
Thornton Dale	62c
Thorpeness	41d
Thrapston	30a
Thropton	67b
Thursby	65d
Thurso	101a
Ticehurst	13c
Tichfield	10c
Tickhill	48a
Tighnabruach	78d
Tilbury	20c
Tillicoultry	81c
Timberscombe	6b
Tintagel	5c
Tintern	15a
Tiptree	22c
Tipton	35d
Tiverton	7a
Tobermory	83d
Toddington	30c
Todhills	87d
Todmorden	53c
Tolleshunt D'Arcy	20b
Tolob	104c
Tomatin	93d
Tomintoul	94c
Tomnavoulin	94c
Tonbridge	13a
Tongland	64d
Tongue	100b
Tonyrefail	24c
Topcliffe	54a
Topsham	4b
Torcross	4c
Torgyle	91d
Torksey	49a
Torpoint	3d
Torquay	4c

Torridon	90b
Torryburn	81d
Torver	57d
Toscaig	90c
Totland	9d
Totnes	4c
Totton	9b
Towcester	29b
Tow Law	60a
Tranent	74b
Trantlebeg	100c
Traquair	74d
Trawsfynydd	33a
Tredegar	24b
Tredington	28d
Treen	1c
Trefriw	44a
Tregaron	25b
Tregony	2c
Trelech	22a
Tremadog	44c
Tresla	104a
Tricketts Cross	9c
Trimdon	60b
Tring	18a
Trochry	86d
Troed-y-thiw	24a
Troon	71d
Trowbridge	16c
Trowse Newton	42a
Trumpington	31a
Truro	2a
Tufton	21b
Tullibody	80d
Tumble	22d
Turnberry	71d
Turrif	96a
Tutbury	36a
Tuxford	48d
Twickenham	18d
Twycross	36d
Twyford (Berks)	18a
Twyford (Hants)	10a
Twyn-Llanan	23b
Twynholm	64c
Tydd St.Mary	38b
Tywyn	33c

U

Uckfield	12a
Ufford	41b
Uig	89b

Ulceby	56c
Ullapool	97a
Ulpha	57d
Ulverston	51b
Umberleigh	6a
Upavon	16d
Upminster	19b
Upper Broughton	37b
Uppingham	37d
Upstreet	14a
Upton	28c
Urchfont	16c
Urmston	46b
Usk	15a
Uttoxeter	36a
Uxbridge	18b
Uyeasound	104b

V

Vange	20a
Ventnor	10c
Verwood	9a
Voe	104a

W

Waddington (Lancs)	52a
Waddington (Lincs)	49d
Wadebridge	2a
Wadhurst	13c
Wainfleet	50d
Wakefield	54c
Wakes Colne	32c
Walberswick	41d
Walkerburn	74d
Wallasey	45b
Wallingford	17b
Walls	104a
Wallsend	68d
Walmer	14b
Walpole	41d
Walsall	36c
Walsingham	40a
Waltham	50a
Waltham Abbey	19b
Waltham Cross	19a
Walton-on-the-Naze	32d
Wantage	17a
Warboys	38d
Warcop	59b
Wardington	29a
Ware	31c

Wareham	9c	Westgate on Sea	14b
Wargrave	18a	Westhoughton	46a
Warley	36c	West Kilbride	71b
Warlingham	19c	West Lavington	16c
Warmington	29a	West Linton	74a
Warminster	16c	West Lulworth	8c
Warning	13c	West Malling	20c
Warrington	46a	West Meon	10a
Warslow	47d	West Mersea	32c
Warter	55b	Westmeston	12c
Warton	51d	West Moors	9c
Warwick	28b	Weston (Staffs)	35b
Washford	7a	Weston on the Green	29d
Washington	68c	Weston-super-Mare	15c
Watchet	7a	West Runton	40a
Waterlooville	10a	West Witton	60c
Watford	18b	Wetheral	66c
Wath Brow	57a	Wetherby	54a
Wath-upon-Dearne	48a	Weybourne	40a
Watlington	17b	Weybridge	18d
Watten	101b	Weymouth	8c
Watton	39d	Whaleybridge	47a
Watton	42a	Whalley	52c
Wear Head	59b	Wharram-le-Street	55b
Weaverham	46c	Whickham	68c
Weaverthorpe	55b	Whiddon Down	6c
Wedmore	15c	Whiltingham	76c
Weedon Bec	29b	Whipsnade	30c
Weeford	36c	Whitbeck	57d
Weem	86d	Whitburn	68d
Weeting	39d	Whitby	62a
Wellingborough	30a	Whitchurch (Hants)	17d
Wellington (Somerset)	7a	Whitchurch (Salop)	35a
Wellington (Salop)	35a	Whitehall	101d
Wells (Somerset)	15d	Whitehaven	57a
Wells (Norfolk)	39b	Whitehills	95b
Welshampton	34b	Whithorn	64c
Welshpool	34a	Whiting Bay	70d
Welwyn Garden City	19a	Whitland	22c
Wem	35a	Whitley Bay	68d
Wemyss Bay	71b	Whitney	17a
Wendens Ambo	31d	Whitstable	14a
Wendlebury	29d	Whitstone	5d
Wendover	18a	Whittington	58c
Wentbridge	54c	Whittlesey	38d
West Auckland	61a	Whitton Gilbert	68c
West Bridgford	37a	Whittonstall	58c
West Bromwich	36c	Wibsey	53d
West Burton	59d	Wick	101a
Westbury	16c	Wickford	20a
West Calder	73b	Wickham	10a
West Coker	8a	Wickham Market	41b
Westerham	19d	Wickwar	15b

Widecombe	4a	Woodbridge	41a
Widnes	46a	Woodchurch	13d
Wigan	46a	Woodford	19b
Wigston	37c	Woodhall Spa	50c
Wigton	65d	Woodstock	29c
Wigtown	64c	Woodyates	9a
Wilby	41b	Woofferton	27a
Willingdon	12d	Wool	8d
Willingham	31a	Woolacombe	5b
Willington	60a	Wooler	76c
Williton	7a	Woolwich	19b
Wilmslow	46b	Wooton Basset	16b
Wilsontown	73b	Worbrough	48a
Wilton	9a	Worcester	28a
Wimborne Minster	9c	Workington	57a
Wincanton	8a	Worksop	48a
Winchcombe	28c	Worle	15c
Winchelsea	13d	Wormit	82a
Winchester	10a	Worthen	34d
Windermere	58c	Worthing	11d
Windsor	18c	Wotton under Edge	16a
Wingham	14a	Wragby	49b
Winkfield	18c	Wrangle	50c
Winkleigh	6c	Wrexham	45d
Winsford	46c	Writtle	20a
Winslow	29d	Wrotham Heath	20c
Winster	57c	Wroxham	42b
Winterbourne (Avon)	15b	Wybunbury	46c
Winterbourne Abbas	8c	Wych Cross	12a
Winterbourne Stoke	9a	Wylye	9a
Winteringham	55d	Wymondham	42a
Wirksworth	47d		
Wisbech	38d	**Y**	
Wisborough Green	11b		
Wishaw	73b	Yarcombe	7b
Witham	32c	Yardley Gobion	29d
Witheridge	6d	Yarm	60b
Withernsea	56d	Yarmouth	9d
Withington	46b	Yatton	15c
Withleigh	6d	Yaxley	38c
Wittersham	13d	Yeadon	53d
Witton-le-Wear	60a	Yealmpton	3d
Wiveliscombe	7a	Yelverton	3b
Wivenhoe	32c	Yeovil	8a
Woking	18d	Yetholm	76c
Wokingham	18c	Yetts of Muckart	81d
Wollaston	30a	York	54b
Wolsingham	60a	Youlgreave	47d
Wolverhampton	35d	Ysbyty Ystwyth	25b
Wolverton	17d	Ystalyfera	23b
Wombwell	48a	Ystradgynlais	23b

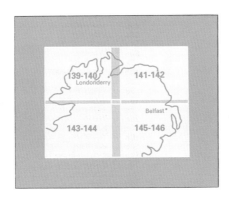

KEY

motorway		car ferry
junction number		railway station
dual carriageway		airport
primary route		canal
'A' road	436 718	height in metres
'B' road		national boundary
other road		county boundary
border crossing point		abbey, ancient monument

Tory Island

T o r y   S o u n d   Horn Head

Inishbofin

Bloody Foreland

(N56)

R257

Falcarragh

Gweedore

Gortahork

Cre

Gola I.

Derrybeg

Owey I.

Bunbeg   R253   Gweedore

R251   Errigal

R251   Glen

^ 752

Rosses
Bay

L. Nacung

Annagry

Natio

The
Rosses

Aran
Island

Burtonport   (N56)

L. Anure

Derryveagh Mts   L

Slieve Snacht
683

R254

R

R259

Crohy Hd

Dungloe

R252

Doochary

Croaghleheen
383 ^   Fintown

D . . . N

Gweebarra
Bay

L. Finn

^ Aghla Mt
598

Portnoo   Narin

Lettermacaward

Dawros Hd

Rosbeg   Maas

R250

Loughros More
Bay

Glenties

R261   (N56)

^ 603

^ Slievetooey
444

Ardara

Blue Stack Mts

^ Blue Stack
676

52!

Glen
Bay

^ 353   R262   525

R263

Glencolumbkille

^ 504   Meentullynagarn

L. Eske

n
y   Malin
More   Slieve   (N15)

Carrick

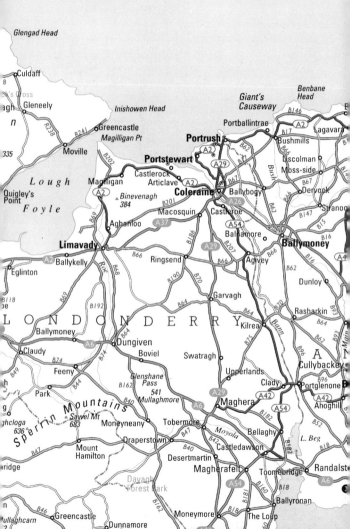

Glengad Head

Culdaff

's Cross

agh   Gleneely

R238   R241   Greencastle   Inishowen Head   Benbane Head

Magilligan Pt   Giant's Causeway   B146

335   Moville   B207   Portballintrae   A2   Lagavara

Bushmills   B17

Portrush   A2   B66   Liscolman

Portstewart   A2   Moss-side   B67

Lough   Castlerock   Articlave   A29   B67   Dervock

Magilligan   B201   **Coleraine**   Ballybogy   B63   Stranoc

Quigley's Point   A2   △ Binevenagh 384   A26   Castleroe   B147   B15

Foyle   B69   Macosquin   A37   **Ballymoney**   B16

Aghanloo   A54   Ballinamore   A4

Limavady   A29   B207   B16

A2   Ballykelly   B66   Ringsend   B66   Agivey   B62

Eglinton   B68   B190   B70   Dunloy

B118   B192   Garvagh   B64   B70   Rasharkin   B64

L O N D O N D E R R Y   Kilrea   B64   B92

Ballymoney   B64   B96   A

Claudy   B74   Dungiven   Boviel   Swatragh   Bann   Cullybackey

B49   B874   Feeny   B44   Upperlands   B96   Portglenone

Park   Glenshane Pass   541   Clady   A42   Ahoghill

hchloga   Mullaghmore   A6   Maghera   A54   B52

636   Sperrin Mountains   Sawel Mt 683   Moneyneany   Tobermore   B47   Moyola   Bellaghy   L. Beg   B18

Draperstown   B40   B42   Castledawson   B182

Mount Hamilton   Desertmartin   **Magherafelt**   Toomebridge   A6   Randalst

ridge   Davagh Forest Park   A54   B160   B18   B

B46   Greencastle   Dunnamore   B162   Moneymore   The Loup   **Ballyronan**

llaghcarn

△ 353

L. Eske

Bay

Glencolumbkille

R263

Malin More

Slieve League △ 601

Carrick

Kilcar

R263

△ 504

Meentullynagarn

Crownarad △ 494

Oily

Inver

Mountcharles

Donegal

N56

N15

Laghey

Killybegs

Dunkineely

Inver Bay

Fintragh Bay

Muckross Head

McSwynes Bay

St John's Pt

Doorin Pt

Rossnowlagh

Coolmore

Ballintra

R23

N15

D o n e g a l   B a y

Mullaghmore Hd

Mullaghmore

Inishmurray

Streedagh Pt

R279

Cliffoney

Kinlough

Creevykeel Court Cairn

R280

△ 522

Lough Melvin

Ballyshannon

Bundoran

Belleek

Erne

A47

A46

R230

B52

Garrison

Rossinver

B52

Scribbagh

Roskeeragh Pt

Grange

N15

Benbulbin △ 525

Dartry Mts

Truskmore 643

Glenade L.

R287

Kiltyclogher

Dough Mt △ 461

Carney

Drumcliff Bay

Drumcliff

High Cross Round Tower

Glencar L.

R280

go

y

Rosses Point

Coney I.

R291

N16

Abbey

L E I T R I M

Shanvus

Manorhamilton

N16

B

Aughris Hd

est

Dromard

N59

Beltra

Strandhill

Carrowmore

Sligo (Sligeach)

R292

R286

L. Gill

Leckaun

R280

Glenfarne

R207

Knocklalongy △ 542

Ballysadare Bay

Ballisodare

Collooney

Abbey

Dromahair

R287

Kilargue

Belhavel L.

Dowra

Shannon

I S G O

untains

Collaney

Toberscanavan

Owenmore

N7

R293

Unshin

R284

Drumkeeran

R200

Lough Allen

Iron

Riverstown

oonacool

Templehouse L.

Ballymote

N4

Lough Arrow

R285

Ballyfarnan

Sl 58

Cross

Tubbercurry

R294

Bunnanadden

R296

R293

Carrowkeel

R295

Ballinafad

Keadue

Drumshan

R280

R208

N17

Doocastle

L. Key

leitrim

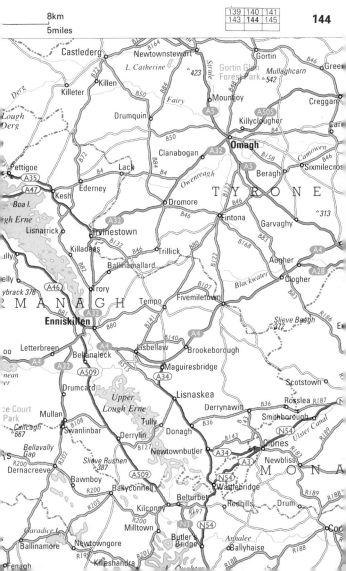

Forest Park

B46 Greencastle
hcarn
Moneymore
Ballyronan
The Loup
B18
B18
Dunnamore
Ballinderry
B162
Creggan
A505
A53
Coagh
Cookstown
B73
Newport
Trench
Kildress
B73
Lough
Ald
Carrickmore
A29
Tullyhogue
B160
B161
Neagh
O N E
Pomeroy
B4
B160
B520
Stewartstown
Camowen
B46
B4
Sixmilecross
B43
Donaghmore
Coalisland
Maghery
Low
Ball
Castlecaulfield
A45
Dungannon
B196
Derrytrasna
▲313
Moygashel
M1
14
Ac
A4
15
B106
13
B131
12
11
10
A76
Ballygawley
B45
B130
Moy
B28
A4
M12
Craigavon
Lu
A4
A28
A5
Charlemont
B28
B77
Portadown
Aughnacloy
B128
Benburb
Blackwater
Loughgall
Bann
gher
Dyan
B128
B131
Richhill
A27
A50
Gilford
A51
B115
Callan
B77
R186
Killylea
Armagh
Hamiltonsbawn
A51
Handrage
Beagh
Emyvale
Caledon
B45
A R M
A G H
Scarva
Glaslough
B110
Milford
A3
Poyntz
New
B183
Markethill
Pass
Canc
Tydavnet
Middletown
B133
B134
otstown
Tyholland
Keady
B132
Mount Norris
R186
Monaghan
assagh
B31
A28
A77
slea R187
(Muineachán)
B3
B8
Whitecross
N54
N2
Clontibret
B32
Darkley
Bessbrook
gh
Cavanagarven
Carnagh
Belleek
Ister Canal
R189
Scotch
Corner
R181
R182
Newtownhamilton
A25
A25
Meigh
A1
M O N A G H A N
R184
A29
Culyhanna
B30
B134
R189
Ballybay
R183
Jonesborough
Or
R188
Rockcorry
R162
Castleblayney
Muckno L.
B35
B30
Crossmaglen
Forkhill
N1
Cootehill
R190
L. Egish
Cullaville
Drumbilla
R177
R192
Shantonagh
R181
Broomfield
N2
N53
De
Sillan L.
Pr

Northern Ireland Index

This index comprises a selection of town and village names in
Northern Ireland. It does not include any Republic of Ireland names
covered by the mapping.
The reference number refers to the page,
and the letter refers to the section of the
map in which the index entry can be found,
as divided into **a**, **b**, **c** and **d** thus:

A

Aghalee	**145b**
Aghanloo	**141a**
Agivey	**141b**
Ahoghill	**141d**
Aldergrove	**146a**
Annalong	**146c**
Annsborough	**146c**
Antrim	**142c**
Ardglass	**146d**
Ardstraw	**140d**
Armagh	**145d**
Armoy	**141b**
Articlave	**141a**
Artigarvan	**140d**
Augher	**144b**
Aughnacloy	**145a**

B

Ballinamallard	**144a**
Ballintoy	**141b**
Ballybogy	**141b**
Ballycarry	**142d**
Ballycastle	**142a**
Ballyclare	**142c**
Ballygalley	**142c**
Ballygawley	**145a**
Ballyhalbert	**146b**
Ballykelly	**141a**
Ballymagorry	**140d**
Ballymartin	**146c**
Ballymena	**142c**
Ballymoney	**141b**
Ballymoney	**141c**
Ballynahinch	**146a**
Ballynure	**142c**
Ballyronan	**141d**
Ballyvoy	**142a**
Ballywalter	**146b**
Ballyward	**146c**
Balnamore	**141c**
Banbridge	**146c**
Bangor	**146b**
Belcoo	**144c**

Belfast	**146a**
Bellaghy	**141d**
Bellanaleck	**144c**
Belleek	**143b**
Belleek	**145d**
Benburb	**145a**
Beragh	**144b**
Bessbrook	**145d**
Blackwater	**145b**
Boviel	**141c**
Brookeborough	**144d**
Broughshane	**142c**
Bushmills	**141b**

C

Caledon	**145c**
Carnagh	**145c**
Carnduff	**142a**
Carnlough	**142c**
Carrickfergus	**142d**
Carrickmore	**144b**
Carryduff	**146a**
Castlecauldfield	**145a**
Castledawson	**141d**
Castlederg	**140c**
Castlerock	**141a**
Castleroe	**141b**
Castlewellan	**146c**
Charlemont	**145b**
Clady	**141d**
Clady	**140c**
Clanabogan	**144b**
Claudy	**140d**
Clogher	**144b**
Cloghy	**146b**
Clough	**146d**
Clough Mills	**141d**
Coagh	**145b**
Coalisland	**145b**
Coleraine	**141b**
Comber	**146b**
Conlig	**146b**
Connor	**142c**
Cookstown	**145a**

Corkey	142c	Garvaghy	144b	
Craig	140d	Gilford	145d	
Craigavad	146b	Glarryford	141d	
Craigavon	145b	Glenariff	142a	
Crawfordsburn	146b	Glenarm	142c	
Creggan	144b	Glenavy	146a	
Crossgar	146b	Glynn	142a	
Crossmaglen	145d	Gortin	140d	
Crumlin	146a	Gracehill	141d	
Cullybackey	141d	Greencastle	141c	
Cullyhanna	145d	Greencastle	146c	
Culmore	140b	Greenisland	142d	
Cushendall	141a	Greyabbey	146b	
Cushendun	142a	Groomsport	146b	
D		**H**		
Darkley	145d	Hamiltonsbawn	145d	
Derrygonnelly	144a	Helen's Bay	146b	
Derrylin	144c	Hillsborough	146a	
Derrynawilt	144d	Hilltown	146c	
Derrytrasna	145b	Holywood	146a	
Dervock	141b	**I**		
Desertmartin	141d	Irvinestown	144a	
Doagh	142c	**J**		
Donagh	144b	Jonesborough	145d	
Donaghadee	146b	**K**		
Donaghcloney	146a	Keady	145d	
Donaghmore	145a	Kells	142c	
Douglas Bridge	140d	Kesh	144a	
Downpatrick	146d	Kildress	145a	
Draperstown	141c	Kilkeel	146c	
Dromard	146a	Killadeas	144a	
Dromore	144b	Killen	144a	
Dromore	146a	Killeter	144a	
Drumahoe	140d	Killinchy	146b	
Drumaness	146c	Killough	146d	
Drumcard	144c	Killyclougher	144b	
Drumquin	144a	Killylea	145c	
Dundonald	146b	Killyleagh	146b	
Dundrum	146c	Kilrea	141d	
Dungannon	145a	Kilwaughter	142c	
Dungiven	141c	Kirkcubbin	146b	
Dunloy	141d	**L**		
Dunmurry	146a	Lack	144a	
Dunnamanagh	140d	Lagavard	141b	
Dunnamore	145a	Larne	142d	
Dyan	145a	Lawrencetown	145b	
E		Letterbreen	144c	
Ederney	144a	Limavady	141a	
Eglinton	140d	Lisbellaw	144d	
Enniskillen	144c	Lisburn	146a	
F		Liscolman	141b	
Feeny	141c	Lisnarrick	144a	
Fintona	144b	Lisnaskea	144d	
Fivemiletown	144b	Londonderry	140d	
Forkhill	145d	Loughbrickland	145d	
G		Loughgall	145b	
Garrison	143b	Loughlinisland	146c	
Garvagh	141d	Lower Ballinderry	146a	

Lurgan	145b	Portmuck	142d
M		Portrush	141b
Macosquin	141b	Portstewart	141b
Maghera	141d	Poyntz Pass	145d
Magherafelt	141d	**R**	
Magheralin	146a	Randalstown	141d
Magheramason	140d	Rasharkin	141d
Maghery	145b	Rathfriland	146c
Magilligan	141a	Richhill	145d
Maguiresbridge	144d	Ringsend	141b
Markethill	145d	Rosslea	144d
Mayobridge	146c	Rostrevor	146c
Meigh	145d	**S**	
Middletown	145c	Saintfield	146a
Milford	145d	Saul	146d
Millisle	146b	Scarva	145d
Milltown	146c	Scotstown	145c
Moira	146a	Scribbagh	143b
Moneymore	141d	Seapatrick	145d
Moneyneany	141c	Shrigley	146b
Moneyreagh	146a	Sion Mills	140d
Moorfields	142c	Six Road Ends	146b
Moss-side	141b	Sixmilecross	144b
Mossley	142c	Stewartstown	145b
Mount Hamilton	141c	Strabane	140d
Mount Norris	145d	Strangford	146d
Mountjoy	144b	Stranocum	141b
Moy	145b	Swatragh	141d
Moygashel	145a	**T**	
Mullan	144c	Tandragee	145d
N		Tassagh	145d
New Buildings	140d	Templepatrick	142c
Newcastle	146c	Tempo	144d
Newport Trench	145b	The Loup	141d
Newry	145d	The Sheddings	142c
Newtown Crommelin	142c	Tobermore	141d
Newtownabbey	146a	Toomebridge	141d
Newtownards	146b	Trillick	144a
Newtownbutler	144d	Trory	144a
Newtownhamilton	145d	Tully	144a
Newtownstewart	140d	Tully	144d
Nutt's Corner	146a	Tullyhogue	145a
O		**U**	
Omagh	144b	Upper Ballinderry	146a
P		Upperlands	141d
Park	140d	**W**	
Pettigoe	144a	Waringstown	145d
Plumbridge	140d	Warrenpoint	146c
Pomeroy	145a	Waterside	140d
Portadown	145b	Wattlebridge	144d
Portaferry	146b	Whitecross	145d
Portavogie	146b	Whitehead	142d
Portballintrae	141b	Whitehouse	146a
Portglenone	141d		

TOWN
PLANS

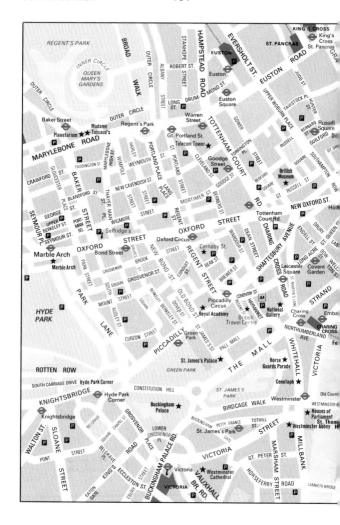

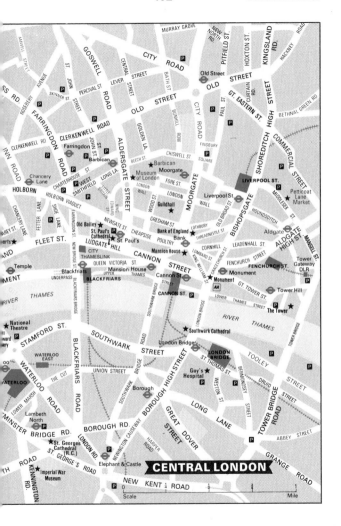

CENTRAL LONDON

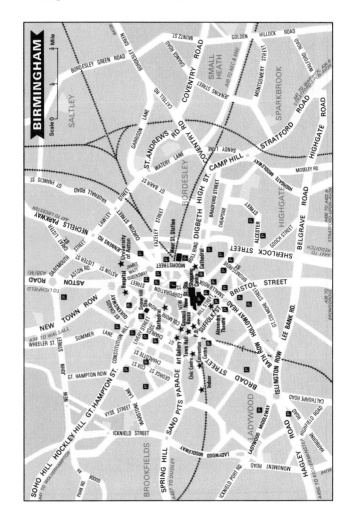

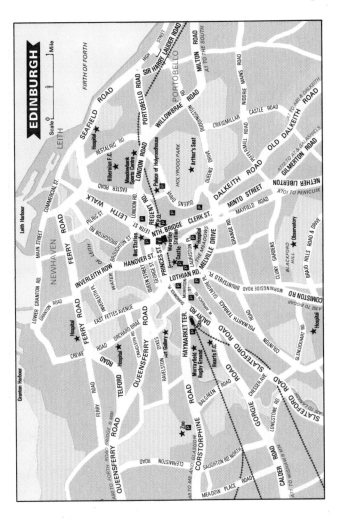

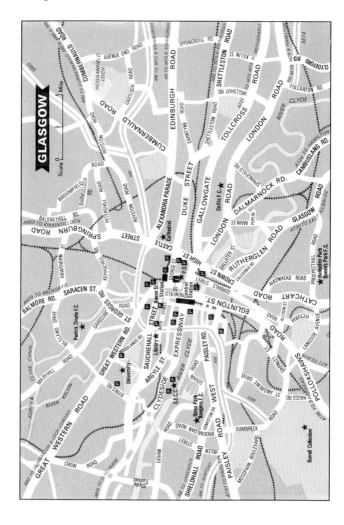

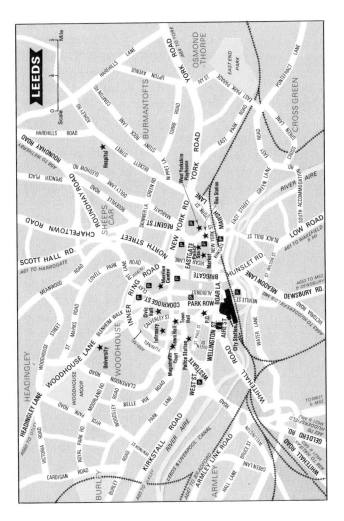

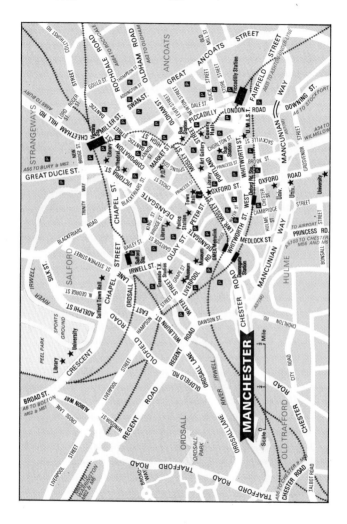

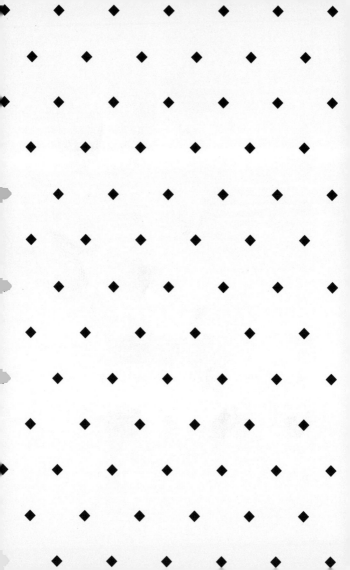